HELPING OTHERS ENGAGE IN NEEDED SERVICES: A POCKET RESOURCE FOR PEER SUPPORT SPECIALISTS AND OUTREACH WORKERS

HELPING OTHERS ENGAGE IN NEEDED SERVICES: A POCKET RESOURCE FOR PEER SUPPORT SPECIALISTS AND OUTREACH WORKERS

Charles Drebing, PhD

For information about permission to reproduce selections from
this book, write to:

Alderson Press, LLC
4217 Wellington Drive
Fort Collins, CO 80526

Library of Congress Cataloging in Publication Data
Drebing, Charles, 1959–
Helping Others Engage in Needed Services: A Pocket Resource
for Peer Support Specialists and Outreach Workers / by Charles
E. Drebing

ISBN 979-8-869-22086-7

To the Peer Support Specialists, outreach workers, and family
and friends who work tirelessly to help others find a way
forward.

CONTENTS

PREFACE

So much research focuses on improving the quality of professional mental healthcare services. While that is appropriate, I wish as much attention was paid to the issue of how to help people engage in those services in a timely way. People usually wait years before they enter needed formal professional treatment for mental health and substance use conditions that are damaging their lives. Many others avoid participating in beneficial community peer support, including self-help groups and one-on-one support. While some recover without these supports, it is clear that many others suffer a great deal of damage to their lives by waiting too long to seek help. We can develop the most effective treatments and supports possible, but if the people who need them wait years before they are willing to try them, what is their real value?

There has been growing interest in how professionals can encourage people to enter needed services. One of the challenges is that healthcare professionals are not really the right individuals to effectively speak to people's ambivalence about getting help. When people feel ambivalent about starting mental health treatment, the ambivalence usually extends to treatment providers. If I don't want to enter therapy or take medications, having a psychologist or psychiatrist tell me I should is not persuasive. What is much more persuasive is having someone—a peer—who has struggled with similar problems and successfully recovered from them talk to me about my concerns about getting help. A peer has the credibility and inside knowledge of what I am feeling, and can be particularly persuasive.

Peer Support Specialists are finding their way into those types of conversations, but not frequently enough. Organizations should be capitalizing on the special credibility that Peer Support Specialists have, and placing them in contact with people who are struggling with the decision of whether to enter care. Maybe organizations are simply too busy providing care to those who have entered to worry about those who have not. Possibly they are just not aware of the needs of those who have not come to their front door yet. Whatever the reason, it is clearly costly for these organizations to ignore the needs of people who are too ambivalent about care and recovery to fully engage. The results include continued suffering and decline in functioning and confidence for the person, and higher costs to the healthcare industry, as people who wait to seek help require more treatment when they eventually do seek out care.

Given your role either as a Peer Support Specialist or outreach worker, it is important that you have the best information and tools possible to ensure you can help people make good decisions about getting help. This is a relatively new challenge, and so you may have to develop your own strategies for this work. My hope, however, is that by sharing some of the tools that do help others make good decisions, your ability to help others will be enhanced.

I wish you the best of luck in your important work and welcome feedback about any other information or resources that should be included in a future edition of this book.

Charles Drebing, PhD

March 2024

CEDrebing@gmail.com

ACKNOWLEDGMENTS

Special thanks to a host of veterans at the Cheyenne VA Medical Center who have shown me so many creative ways that peer support can add to effective healthcare. Michael Moore, Michelle Kane, Eric Dickson, Jon Levy, Jason LaRose, Deni Darby, Buddy Patterson, Jeremy Kilpatrick, and Trina Chew are just a few of those whose work as Peer Support Specialists has been a source of inspiration for this book. Additional thanks to Heather Rodino for her editorial assistance.

HOW TO USE THIS BOOK

This book is designed to be a practical resource to build your skills in helping others enter either professional mental health/substance use services or community-based peer support. Peer support providers are uniquely positioned to help people move past feeling ambivalent to making informed decisions about engaging support, and then taking action. While peer support providers, and specifically Peer Support Specialists, are finding many ways that they can contribute to the recovery of others, this specific area of engagement may be the most important of all. If you are an outreach worker, this book should be helpful to you as well. Your job is evidence that organizations are recognizing the need for dedicated outreach. Hopefully, this book has strategies and tools that will help you be more effective in this work.

As a mental health clinician, I have worked with so many people who waited years to enter treatment. In almost every case, the individual would have benefited from earlier treatment, with most paying a heavy price for waiting. The cost to these clients, their families, the community, and the healthcare system is often very high. This book is an effort to help Peer Support Specialists and outreach workers understand these situations and to offer them effective tools to help people make timely decisions about getting help.

It is important to acknowledge that I am not a Peer Support Specialist. I have personal experience of the impact of mental illness in my own life and in my family, but I have not worked in the role of a peer. This book reflects my own perspective as a mental health program manager and researcher. Peer Support Specialists will hopefully add their own perspective to this important area of work.

The book is divided into several large sections.

The chapters in Part I focus on the common themes around people's decision to enter or not to enter support or treatment. The goal for this section is to build a foundation for understanding how people make those decisions.

Chapters in Part II focus on specific tools that you can use to help people make better decisions. Each of these chapters takes a theory or set of techniques and describes them in sufficient detail to allow you to include them in your work with clients. There are many tools described here—more than you can fully digest in any one reading. I would encourage you to read one chapter at a time, focusing on each tool until you feel you've incorporated it before trying to add others. I find that I often have to read about theories three to four times before I really feel that I understand them and can use them to guide my actions. While there are a lot of tools peers and outreach workers can use, these chapters will provide you with a range of core strategies for being helpful.

Chapters in Part III are designed to provide important information about specific clinical needs (substance use, suicidal ideation, etc.) your clients may face. Each chapter will tell you briefly about these needs, how they commonly appear and change over time, and associated patterns in how people enter and use care. You will also find information you can use in conversation with clients. For example, information about the long-term health costs for each clinical need can assist clients in making better decisions about seeking help.

Appendix A contains a helpful summary of strategies for working with clients who are in crisis and/or need immediate help to stay safe. In your work with people who have not yet sought help, it is likely you may come across someone in crisis and so this appendix should be a quick guide for you.

Appendix B contains helpful quotes related to making changes. I often find that the right quote, shared at a key moment in conversation, can help others decide to make a change. Read through these quotes and find those that feel meaningful and useful to you. Revisit them occasionally, as you may find that what is useful changes as you get more involved with helping people find help.

This book is not meant to replace information you will need for a specific job or volunteer role that you may hold. Nor is it a substitute for learning the guidelines and policies of the organization you work for. It does, however, include background and skill-specific information to help you continue your growth in this strategically important work. As a Peer Support Specialist or outreach worker, you should be part of a team, and your team will also have a part in this work. You will want to approach this effort in a way that involves effective team work—and so this book includes tools that you might use as you play your part on your team.

PART I: UNDERSTANDING THE CHALLENGE

CHAPTER 1

RECOVERY, PEER SUPPORT, AND TREATMENT

The terms *recovery*, *peer support*, and *treatment* are central to the work you do. And yet people use these terms in different ways, leading to unnecessary confusion. We will start by defining the way we'll use these terms in this discussion.

RECOVERY

There is a great deal of discussion and debate about the term *recovery*. For our purposes, we will use the definition offered by the Substance Abuse and Mental Health Services Administration (SAMHSA). SAMHSA defines recovery as "a process of change through which individuals improve their health and wellness, live a self-directed life, and strive to reach their full potential." They go on to spotlight ten key elements (SAMSHA, 2024a):

1.	**Recovery Emerges from Hope.** The belief that recovery is real provides the essential and motivating message of a better future—that people can and do overcome the internal and external challenges, barriers, and obstacles that confront them. Hope is internalized and can be fostered by peers, families, providers, allies, and others. Hope is the catalyst of the recovery process.

2.	**Recovery Is Person-Driven.** Self-determination and self-direction are the foundations for recovery as individuals define their own life goals and design their unique path(s) towards those goals. Individuals optimize their autonomy and independence to the greatest extent possible by leading, controlling, and exercising choice over the services and supports that assist their recovery and resilience. In so doing, they are empowered and provided the resources to make informed decisions, initiate recovery, build on their strengths, and gain or regain control over their lives.

3.	**Recovery Occurs Via Many Pathways.** Individuals are unique with distinct needs, strengths, preferences, goals, culture, and backgrounds—including trauma experience—that affect and determine their pathway(s) to recovery. Recovery is built on the multiple capacities, strengths, talents, coping abilities, resources, and inherent value of each individual. Recovery pathways are highly personalized. They may include professional clinical treatment; use of medications; support from families and in schools; faith-based approaches; peer support; and other approaches. Recovery is non-linear, characterized by continual growth and improved functioning that may involve setbacks. Because setbacks are a natural, though not inevitable, part of the recovery process, it is essential to foster resilience for all individuals and families. Abstinence from the use of alcohol, illicit drugs, and non-prescribed medications is the goal for those with addictions.

Use of tobacco and nonprescribed or illicit drugs is not safe for anyone. In some cases, recovery pathways can be enabled by creating a supportive environment. This is especially true for children, who may not have the legal or developmental capacity to set their own course.

4.   **Recovery Is Holistic.** Recovery encompasses an individual's whole life, including mind, body, spirit, and community. This includes addressing: self-care practices, family, housing, employment, transportation, education, clinical treatment for mental disorders and substance use disorders, services and supports, primary healthcare, dental care, complementary and alternative services, faith, spirituality, creativity, social networks, and community participation. The array of services and supports available should be integrated and coordinated.

5.   **Recovery Is Supported by Peers and Allies.** Mutual support and mutual aid groups, including the sharing of experiential knowledge and skills, as well as social learning, play an invaluable role in recovery. Peers encourage and engage other peers and provide each other with a vital sense of belonging, supportive relationships, valued roles, and community. Through helping others and giving back to the community, one helps one's self. Peer-operated supports and services provide important resources to assist people along their journeys of recovery and wellness. Professionals can also play an important role in the recovery process by providing clinical treatment and other services that support individuals in their chosen recovery paths. While peers and allies play an important role for many in recovery, their role for children and youth may be slightly different. Peer supports for families are very important for children with behavioral health problems and can also play a supportive role for youth in recovery.

6.   **Recovery Is Supported Through Relationship and Social Networks.** An important factor in the recovery process is the presence and involvement of people who believe in the person's ability to recover; who offer hope, support, and encouragement; and who also suggest strategies and resources for change. Family members, peers, providers, faith groups, community members, and other allies form vital support networks. Through these relationships, people leave unhealthy and/or unfulfilling life roles behind and engage in new roles (e.g., partner, caregiver, friend, student, employee) that lead to a greater sense of belonging, personhood, empowerment, autonomy, social inclusion, and community participation.

7.   **Recovery Is Culturally Based and Influenced.** Culture and cultural background in all of its diverse representations—including values, traditions, and beliefs—are keys in determining a person's journey and unique pathway to recovery. Services should be culturally grounded, attuned, sensitive, congruent, and competent, as well as personalized to meet each individual's unique needs.

8.   **Recovery Is Supported by Addressing Trauma.** The experience of trauma (such as physical or sexual abuse, domestic violence, war, disaster, and others) is often a precursor to or associated with alcohol and drug use, mental health problems, and related issues. Services and supports should be trauma-informed to foster safety (physical and emotional) and trust, as well as promote choice, empowerment, and collaboration.

9.   **Recovery Involves Individual, Family, and Community Strengths and Responsibility.** Individuals, families, and communities have strengths and resources that serve as a foundation for recovery. In addition, individuals have a personal responsibility for their own self-care and journeys of recovery. Individuals should be supported in

speaking for themselves. Families and significant others have responsibilities to support their loved ones, especially for children and youth in recovery. Communities have responsibilities to provide opportunities and resources to address discrimination and to foster social inclusion and recovery. Individuals in recovery also have a social responsibility and should have the ability to join with peers to speak collectively about their strengths, needs, wants, desires, and aspirations.

10.   **Recovery Is Based on Respect.** Community, systems, and societal acceptance and appreciation for people affected by mental health and substance use problems—including protecting their rights and eliminating discrimination—are crucial in achieving recovery. There is a need to acknowledge that taking steps towards recovery may require great courage. Self-acceptance, developing a positive and meaningful sense of identity, and regaining belief in one's self are particularly important.

PEER SUPPORT

Like *recovery*, *peer support* has also been defined in a variety of ways. One commonly used definition is "social/emotional support, frequently coupled with instrumental support (practical support such as giving or loaning money or possessions, or physically helping with a task such as giving a ride to a meeting or helping someone move), that is mutually offered or provided by persons having a mental health condition to others sharing a similar mental health condition to bring about a desired social or personal change" (Solomon, 2004). For our purposes, this definition may be too narrowly focused on mental health. Peer support can happen between anyone, and can include supports for any type of need, including mental health, medical, and needs related to any type of life problem (loss of a loved one, challenges with parenting, financial strain, etc.). The focus on social/emotional support is very useful, and the notion that "instrumental support" can be involved is also helpful. While many people can provide peer support, *Peer Support Specialist* is a job title for someone with personal experience with an illness or health condition, as well as experience in using treatment and with recovery. They use that experience to help others recover and successfully use healthcare and other resources.

Peer support groups, also described as *self-help*, *mutual-aid*, or *mutual-help groups*, refer to a group of people who gather together to talk about shared problems or experiences and to provide informal support to each other. (I will use the terms *peer support group* and *self-help group* interchangeably.) The focus of the group may be a common clinical condition (such as addiction, diabetes, or depression), a life problem (a trauma, loss of child, or bankruptcy), or a personal circumstance or challenge (veterans' groups, those trying to lose weight, or people looking to advance their career).

TREATMENT

For this discussion, we will define *treatment* as any action taken by a healthcare professional as part of efforts to manage, prevent, cure, or slow the progression of a medical or mental health condition. The key for our definition is that these actions are taken by an identified healthcare professional as part of formal care to address an identified health condition. Certified Peer Support Specialists are now considered healthcare professionals in many settings, and so their assistance can be seen as falling under the heading of "treatment." For our discussion, though, it will be most helpful to think of the work of Peer Support Specialists as peer support and not treatment. Again, this is not entirely true, but this distinction will help us in this conversation.

HOW DO RECOVERY, PEER SUPPORT, AND TREATMENT RELATE TO EACH OTHER IN REAL LIFE?

The primary goal of peer support and treatment is to promote recovery. In this way, they are two tools for achieving the same goal and potentially two collaborative efforts to meet that goal. But does it work that way in real life?

We need to go back to the definition of *recovery* to emphasize one of the key elements: recovery varies widely in how it happens. There is no one pathway to recovery and no single strategy that works. Data collected from thousands of people who have achieved recovery document that people recover in a variety of ways. For some, peer support and treatment are key to the process. Others recover without any treatment or any real identifiable peer support. Therefore, we cannot make any assumptions about what people will need to recover. Variation is so common that it is one of the core principles in the definition of recovery.

Unfortunately, common assumptions that people hold about recovery often do not reflect this core reality.

THE MYTH OF GATEKEEPERS

The researcher Keith Humphreys was one of the first to talk about the "gatekeeper myth," pointing to the belief held by many professional clinicians and researchers, and some patients, that "recovery can only be achieved with the assistance of highly trained healthcare professionals" (Humphreys, 2015). This is reflected in what providers say to patients and by what researchers measure and study. If recovery happens only through treatment, then everyone needs treatment, and we need to study people in treatment if we want to understand recovery. Fortunately, there are researchers that have not started with this assumption, and have documented clearly that many people recover without treatment. For example, there is clear evidence that a large portion of adults who recover from a substance use disorder do so without professional treatment (Klingemann, Sobell & Sobell, 2010).

There is a second version of the gatekeeper myth involving peer support. It is harder to find in written documents such as research studies, but it is commonly found in the statements of people involved in peer support groups. In this version, recovery is believed possible only through peer support, or only through specific peer support groups. For example, some laypeople and some providers believe that attendance at 12-step or other peer support group is the only way to recover from a substance use disorder. Again, researchers have shown clearly that this is not the case. If we look at the large studies of how people recover from substance use disorders, a sizeable portion recover without any involvement in peer support groups (Granfield & Cloud, 1996; Toneatto, Sobell, Sobell & Rubel, 1999).

Why do these myths develop, and why do they persist? These are not purposeful lies, but rather illusions that people believe and spread. One likely reason is that many clinicians, peers, and patients are simply drawing conclusions from what they personally experience. If providers see recovery only when it happens in the patients they treat, it makes sense that they will think it happens only in treatment. Similarly, if people attending AA or any other peer support group only see people recover in that setting, it is easy to conclude that recovery is only possible in those settings. **They don't know what they haven't seen.** Relatedly, people tend to overestimate the importance of their own personal experience: "If it worked for me, then it should work for everyone else." It is funny that we fall into this trap; we often don't like it when others assume that what helped them will help us, but then we make the same assumption about others. A third explanation is that these myths are simple, and we like simple strategies. SAMSHA's definition reflects the research data that says that there is no simple, common way that people recover—instead, huge variations exist. It is hard to hold that in our heads and hard to get excited about any process so varied and complex. It is easier instead to emphasize a simple strategy we believe in and push others toward it.

Unfortunately, these myths are not true and are not worth holding on to. First, the reality is that people will find out through their experience that our prescribed pathway does not necessarily work for them. They will find their own way to recover, just as we found our own way to solve our problems, despite the misguided recommendations of others. When we embrace simple myths about recovery, in the end we undermine our own credibility. We may feel confident in the short run by arguing that there is a simple path, but in the long run, many will see us as simplistic or dogmatic, and then will not be interested in what we say. We may also feel that we have more persuasive power with others if we emphasize a simple recipe for recovery— "You have to be in a peer support group," "You have to have a sponsor," "You have to use an evidence-based psychotherapy," or "You have to use this medication"—but there are ways to be persuasive without saying things that are inaccurate. This book includes some tools for helping others recover, but it assumes that you will be willing to give up strategies related to the gatekeeper myths. They are not accurate and, in the long run, not helpful.

SHOULD WE ENCOURAGE PEOPLE TO ENGAGE IN PEER SUPPORT OR TREATMENT?

While treatment and self-help groups aren't the only way to recover, they are helpful for many, and essential for some people.

Researchers who have documented that some people recover without self-help also document that many people do recover with self-help groups and/or treatment, and that self-help groups and treatment are effective in dealing with a wide range of mental health and life problems (Worrall et al., 2018). These same researchers have also found that the people who typically recover without peer support or treatment often have relatively mild versions of the problem they are struggling with. More severe conditions are more likely to require treatment and/or peer support. These studies also have found that those who recover without using treatment or peer support often have more resources—more social support at home, better finances, or more psychological strengths—than those who do not. In contrast, those who do not have as many resources are more likely to need peer support or treatment in order to achieve lasting recovery.

HOW DO TREATMENT AND SELF-HELP RELATE TO EACH OTHER?

Interestingly, there are versions of the gatekeeper's myth that explicitly say, "Only treatment works; self-help groups don't really work" and "Self-help is the only thing that really works; treatment doesn't work." I've heard people state each of these myths. Research clearly shows that neither is true. When researchers look at treatment versus involvement in self-help groups, versus the combination of self-help and treatment, they find that (1) both treatment and self-help groups have clear benefits, and (2) it is the combination that produces the best outcomes. Treatment does not negate self-help and vice versa. If our job is to give people any and every tool that might help them recover, shouldn't we encourage them to consider both treatment and peer support, and let them know that the best outcomes are associated with both?

IN SUMMARY

How we think about these issues of treatment, self-help, and recovery will determine what we say to others and whether we will be of help or potentially be a source of harm. To be clear in how we will approach these issues, this book makes the following assumptions:

- Individuals recover in a variety of ways. Some use no supports, some use peer support, some use professional treatment, and some use a combination of both.

- Individual recovery is primarily the responsibility of the person, *not* the healthcare providers and *not* Peer Support Specialists. The person who needs to recover is ultimately responsible for how they choose to recover.

- Most decisions about using peer support or professional treatment are not made alone. People rely on input from family, friends, and the community to decide how to achieve their recovery.

- Slow engagement and no engagement into peer support and treatment is common and is often costly for the person, their family, and the community.

- Strategies that make it easier to engage in community supports and in treatment in a timely fashion will result in less costly delays and in more people achieving recovery.

- Peer Support Specialists have a unique advantage in helping people successfully engage in community support and treatment.

CHAPTER 2

WHY TIMELY TREATMENT AND COMMUNITY SUPPORT ARE IMPORTANT

We generally assume that people get help when they need to. There is clear evidence this is not true. Significant delays in reaching out for help, either in the form of community support or formal treatment, are common for many clinical conditions, particularly mental illness.

For example, in a large survey of the general population, researchers identified people who had a variety of mental illnesses, and then examined how long it took for them to enter appropriate treatment for the first time (Kessler, Olfson & Berglund, 1998). One of the disorders that was tracked was panic disorder, a fairly uncomfortable anxiety disorder characterized by sudden strong feelings of fear, known as panic attacks, that usually last from five to ten minutes but can last for hours. It often feels like the person is having a heart attack or stroke, leading many people to go to the emergency room. More than 50 percent of adults with panic disorder enter treatment within one year of their first symptoms, and 75 percent within 3 years. Given time, almost everyone who experiences panic disorder will enter treatment for it (Wang et al., 2005).

Contrast that with adults who would meet the criteria for major depression and/or dysthymia. Major depression is a feeling of being down or depressed that lingers for at least two weeks and that is severe enough that it disrupts daily functioning (work, school, relationships, etc.). Depression does not start as abruptly as a panic attack, and symptoms of depression can make you feel apathetic or lethargic about taking any action, including seeking help. Dysthymia is a condition similar to major depression, though the symptoms are typically more chronic and not as severe as major depression. Thirty percent of adults with major depression or dysthymia enter treatment within one year of their first symptoms. It takes seven to eight years before 50 percent of those adults with major depression/dysthymia have entered treatment, and about 10 percent will never enter treatment (Wang et al., 2005a). This is much slower than the entry rate for panic disorder.

When we look at adults who would meet criteria for either drug or alcohol use disorder, only about 10 percent of this group enters treatment within a year of developing these symptoms, and it takes about thirty years for 50 percent to enter treatment. The best data suggest that about 25 percent of adults with an active substance use disorder will never enter treatment (Wang et al., 2005a). This entry rate is much slower than either panic disorder or depression.

These three examples illustrate the following points: (1) how quickly people enter needed treatment varies greatly among disorders, with the most immediately uncomfortable disorders leading to shorter delays; and (2) even when time to treatment is relatively quick, many people wait a substantial amount of time (years) before actually getting treatment.

All of this leads to the key question: What is likely happening while people have symptoms but are not in treatment? It is hard to imagine that those years are not a serious problem. First, people are suffering with symptoms. Those symptoms are almost certainly having a direct impact on their ability to take care of daily demands. They may disrupt work or school. They may interfere with intimate relationships and with the ability to be a successful parent or family member. They may make it more difficult to maintain friendships and live a full, happy life in the community.

In a study in which we looked at people with untreated mental illness over time (Drebing, 2014), we found that as time went on, these untreated symptoms did lead to serious problems at work, at school, and with family life. More importantly, those changes in work and family life then led to more symptoms, which then led to more problems. For example, for one participant, depression led to poor work performance, which caused him to lose his job. His job loss then made his depression much worse, which made it more difficult to look for a new job. This is a common pattern called a "cascading effect," in which problems lead to symptoms and feeling demoralized, which then lead to more problems, which lead to more symptoms. Over time, that cascading effect has a devastating impact on people's lives. In our study we saw many people whose lives moved from a happy family and work life, to job loss and conflict at home, then to divorce and chronic unemployment, with some even moving on to homelessness. For most, these losses took years to accumulate.

One of the more concerning findings was that as people had difficulty being successful at work or school, their families often stepped in to cover those responsibilities for them. Spouses may have taken a new job to replace lost income. Family members made statements that suggested they had lowered their expectations of the person, no longer seeing them as able to work or complete a degree in school. As the families reorganized around the person with untreated mental illness, the person was left with a diminishing role in the family. You can imagine that in such a situation many would conclude that their family members didn't respect or need them as much. Indeed, these individuals reported feeling demoralized, as if their life turned into something they didn't see as valuable.

Interestingly, once families had reorganized around a member with a disabling illness, they were often hesitant to reorganize again around the person when they recovered. We heard repeated examples of family members who were resistant to their relative going back to work. They said things like, "What if it makes them get sick again?" and "I think it is safer if they just stay at home and I work from now on." The process that started with slow entry into needed treatment often ended with lasting disability and stiff challenges to recovery. While we can't prevent many of these illnesses yet, we do have the opportunity to prevent the impact of untreated illness. We have to do more than we are doing now. We have to understand why and how people do and do not enter treatment, and where the best opportunities for encouraging entry are. Here are some of the key factors determining entry.

1. **Seeking Help Is Related to What We Need Help For.** Clear and painful conditions that need treatment (e.g., a broken leg) almost always result in rapid efforts to get help. In contrast, unclear conditions and conditions that don't produce obvious intense pain often don't lead to quick help seeking. Many mental illnesses (e.g.,

depression, anxiety, substance use) fall into this category. People are often not sure what the cause of their symptoms is or if they represent a problem that requires help. They may feel that other demands in life are more important and so they should put off getting help.

2. **Social Stigma.** Problems that are seen by society as undesirable—those that have a stigma associated with them—often lead people to put off acknowledging that they have that problem or that they need help. Again, many mental illnesses fit in this category. We don't want to be seen as having depression or psychosis or any mental illness, and seeking help is a concrete way of acknowledging that we do have a problem.

3. **Conditions That May Clear Without Treatment Are Likely to be Associated with Delays in Help Seeking.** Mental health conditions typically fit in this category. For some, the hope for recovery without treatment is wishful thinking, but for others, this is reasonable, as people wait to see if they really need help.

4. **Lack of Knowledge.** When people don't know what kind of treatment will be needed to address a condition or symptom or don't know how to get that treatment, they often delay seeking help. Again, this is not uncommon for many mental health conditions, as the public still has limited understanding of mental health services. That is also true of peer support and self-help services, as the public often has no understanding of the large support group resources available to them and only finds out about these when the need arises.

To be effective in using treatment or peer support, we need to know about (1) health and disease, (2) treatment/self-help options and how to navigate the healthcare and peer support systems, and (3) the process of recovering from that condition. Researchers refer to this knowledge as mental health literacy (MHL) and define it as the knowledge of mental health disorders that is associated with recognition, management, and prevention. Studies around the world have consistently found that the public has poor MHL (Furnham & Swami, 2018), and that this lack of knowledge is one of the most significant barriers to help seeking and to recovery (Gronholm, Thornicroft, Laurens, & Evans-Lacko, 2017).

5. **Costs of Treatment.** What we know about treatment can impact how quickly we enter it, and if the available treatments are costly in some way, we are more likely to be slow in pursuing them. That is true not only of the financial cost in terms of fees and co-pays, but in terms of travel time and other "expenses" like lost time at work. There is also the discomfort level—some treatments are painful to participate in. For example, some of the best therapies for anxiety disorders can stimulate brief experiences of anxiety as part of the treatment. While discomfort is a different type of "cost," it has the same impact of lowering motivation to participate. It is also true that if we don't think that available treatments are certain to work, then we feel less motivated to do the work to enter treatment. It is not whether the treatment actually works but whether WE THINK the treatment will work. A large difference often exists between what research shows about the effectiveness of current treatments and what the public thinks about their effectiveness. This is also related to the concept of hope. Hopeful people are more likely to think that treatment will help, and thus are more likely to seek help.

6. **Symptoms That Undermine Help Seeking.** With some mental health conditions, the symptoms of the illness actually undermine treatment seeking. For example, in an illness like PTSD, some of the symptoms focus on the avoidance of anything related to the traumatic event, including thoughts and conversations about it. Those symptoms make it more difficult to seek help in which the person will have to talk about the traumatic event as part of treatment. Similarly, substance use disorders involve loss of control of substance use. The thoughts and feelings associated with that substance use will cause resistance to entering treatments that focus on restoring control of substance use.

Depression, one of the most common forms of mental illness, involves symptoms that make it difficult to initiate new actions, and may undermine the concern for one's well-being that usually prompts help seeking. Illnesses that involve psychosis or cognitive deficits like impairments in memory or problem-solving often include impaired self-awareness ("I don't have a problem!") or impaired ability to find help. For all these reasons, help seeking for mental illness is an uphill battle, which causes the common long delays.

FAILING TO SEEK HELP IS ASSOCIATED WITH COMMON "COSTS" TO THE PERSON, THEIR FAMILY, AND THE COMMUNITY

The costs of untreated mental illness can take many shapes. Here are some of the most common:

1. **Extended Symptoms.** Delayed entry into needed treatment and/or support is associated with prolonged suffering. When people with panic disorder or PTSD or depression wait two years to enter treatment, that illness is active for two more years in that person's life, with symptoms that cause them emotional suffering. As we've seen, some people will recover without treatment, but for a large portion of people, delayed treatment results in extended illness.

2. **Functioning.** Delayed entry into treatment is also commonly associated with challenges in and, often, decline in functioning at work and school. Most mental illnesses are associated with problems in functioning, and for most adults, work and school are two such key areas where mental illness has a negative impact, whether it is on the motivation to work, the cognitive ability to do work tasks, or the ability to relate effectively to bosses and coworkers. Over time, significant problems can develop that result in disciplinary action, failure in school, job loss, and unemployment. In our research, we saw many people whose education and work lives were derailed by mental illness in ways that took years to recover from.

    Delayed entry into needed treatment and/or support is also associated with declines in functioning at home. Relationships at home are typically our most important but also our most challenging. Being a successful spouse or parent demands our best. Mental illness often undermines our ability to maintain healthy intimacy and be an effective parent. Years of waiting to get help often extends these problems in ways that raise the risk of long-term damage to marriages and relationships with children, siblings, and partners.

Similarly, negative changes can occur in the roles we play in our extended family, our network of friends, and in our community. As work and family relationships erode over time, we are vulnerable to moving from being a key contributor to someone who relies heavily on the support of others. As mentioned earlier, it is not long before our families and communities reorganize around our struggles so that we have to work very hard to change people's minds if we want to recover our prior roles.

3. **Confidence and Hope.** Delayed entry into needed treatment and/or support is associated with overall damage to morale, slowly undermining our confidence in ourselves and in life. Unchecked symptoms undermine our optimism that we can earn things that we want and that life has good things in store for us. Loss of confidence and hope may be the most devastating cost of all, as our own demoralization causes us to be less likely to try to solve the problems we face.

CHAPTER 3

WHY PEER SUPPORT SPECIALISTS PLAY A KEY ROLE

SAMSHA defines the broad category of *peer support providers* (which includes Peer Support Specialists) as "people who have been successful in the recovery process who help others experiencing similar situations. Through shared understanding, respect, and mutual empowerment, peer support workers help people become and stay engaged in the recovery process and reduce the likelihood of relapse. Peer support services can effectively extend the reach of treatment beyond the clinical setting into the everyday environment of those seeking a successful, sustained recovery process" (SAMSHA, 2024b).

The field of peer support has grown dramatically in the past twenty years, both in the number of people employed as Peer Support Specialists and in the range of settings in which Peer Support Specialists are working. The largest driving force behind this change is the fact that the healthcare system increasingly recognizes the way peer support can solve key challenges. In the US, services run for and by people and their families with serious mental health problems now number more than double the traditional, professionally run mental health organizations (Goldstrom et al., 2006).

WHY IS THE ROLE OF PEER SUPPORT SPECIALIST SO UNIQUE?

1. **You Have Unique Credibility.** In many ways, effective healthcare involves educating and persuading people to make changes related to their health. Clinicians typically complete years of formal graduate training about illness, treatment, and recovery. That knowledge is very useful to people in the patient role. Unfortunately, it is only part of the information patients need. Because Peer Support Specialists have lived experience of an illness, participation in treatment, and recovery, they possess a different type of knowledge: personal experience. It is one thing to hear about the facts of an illness from a trained expert, but it is quite another to hear about the experience of that illness from someone who has lived it. Unlike clinicians, peer workers and Peer Support Specialists are explicitly trained to talk about their personal experience to help others struggling with an illness. That experience gives them a type of credibility that most clinicians do not have.

   When we experience any type of illness, we typically rely on information from a range of sources—family, friends, health workers, and even the media—to figure out how to respond. Each of these sources has some credibility, but they can also have agendas other than simply helping the person. Because of their experience, Peer Support Specialists are typically seen as having a personal connection to the patient, and so more credibility in terms of providing trustworthy guidance.

2. **You Help People Change.** Research on persuasion provides a strong rationale for the special influence of peer support and Peer Support Specialists. For example, people we judge to be more similar to us are more likely to change our views than those who are not as similar (Ruijten, 2021). *Perceived empathy*, defined as "sharing the subjective experience of another person," has been associated with greater potential to persuade (Shen, 2010, 2011). Messages that involve stories as opposed to directives have been associated with more ability to persuade (Moyer-Gusé & Nabi, 2010; Gardner & Leshner, 2016). Messages that emphasize the autonomy of the person and the fact that they have a choice are also more persuasive. All these principles support the view that Peer Support Specialists have clear advantages in influencing others to change.

3. **You Have a Unique "Stance."**
   Your role and relationship to the client gives you several key advantages:
   - As a Peer Specialist, you go through the situation *with* the person. You are not leading them. You are not telling them what to do. Your role is, in large part, to accompany them so that they are not alone.

   - Your focus is on their autonomy, their empowerment. You support their freedom, just as you value your own. At times you may be tempted to try to pressure them into a decision, but you hopefully resist that impulse, valuing their right to make their own decisions.

- You champion person-centered care and shared decision-making. You recognize that healthcare and recovery involve many large and small decisions, and that other people will be involved in those decisions, as others bring information and resources. You consistently support the perspective that all care decisions must be centered around the interests and preferences of the client. Except in the direst situations (e.g., medical emergencies), all those shared decisions are based on the client's choices and preferences.

- As a Peer Support Specialist, you have one overarching agenda: to help your client recover from whatever illness they are facing. You do not pursue your own interests over theirs. You make sure there is no question as to why you are involved and why you are saying or doing anything—it is for your client. This stance leads to the client being more engaged in treatment (Dixon, Holoshitz & Nossel, 2016).

4. **You Have Unique Information That Clients Need.** Clinicians offer important information to patients, including the latest data about illnesses and treatment. They can share patterns they see in their patients with similar problems. But most do not have the personal experience of that illness or that treatment. Even if they do, many will not talk about it openly with patients, as doing so is often seen as inappropriate. This is where Peer Support Specialists bring their personal experience to the clinical setting. Even when they have not had a specific illness or treatment themselves, they are usually

able to talk with clients about similar experiences or share the experiences of other peers who have. When it comes to helping people engage in needed peer support or treatment, the most important information that peers contribute includes:

- The experience of being ill and how that illness appears, and develops or changes over time.

- How people recognize an illness and how they come to the decision to get help.

- The costs and benefits of not getting help in a timely manner.

- The costs and benefits of getting help.

- The experience of engaging in different treatments and what that is like over time.

- The experience of engaging in peer support and self-help resources and what this is like over time.

- The process of recovering and what this is like over time.

RECOVERY STORIES

A common tool used by Peer Support Specialists is the recovery story. This is not a single story, but rather a collection of stories that reflect that peer's experience with illness, treatment, and recovery, as well as the experience of others. Peer Support Specialists use these stories in order to engage, guide, and support clients.

A good recovery story:

1. **Educates.** An effective story includes information that your client can use in their efforts to recognize what they are struggling with and to decide whether they want to seek help and what sort of help. This may be information about the experience of having the illness, using healthcare, using peer support, and the costs and benefits of recovering.

2. **Raises Hope.** A good recovery story demonstrates that it is possible to seek help in a way that results in recovery, and it is possible to take the difficult steps needed to recover. Make sure your stories include a description of the steps that you or others took to get help, and the benefits of taking those steps. Clients often have difficulty imagining themselves in recovery, and so your stories should also include information about what it is like to recover. That doesn't mean your story should ignore the challenges of recovery. Stories that are unrealistically positive are not persuasive and undermine your credibility. Realistic hope recognizes the real challenges of recovery but sees the overall benefit.

3. **Engages.** A good recovery story helps the client connect to you as a person. If you are part of a clinical team, it will help them connect to the team, as the client sees you as a representative of the team. A good story often increases the sense of trust and rapport with that client, creating more openings for you and other clinicians to talk openly about the possibilities of getting help.

COMMON TYPES OF RECOVERY STORIES FOR ENGAGEMENT

You will probably want variations of your recovery stories that focus on different themes, so that you can use these to address the different needs of various audiences. You pick the theme that will most likely be useful for different groups and individuals. Common themes include:

1. **First Recognition of the Problem.** Almost everyone is initially unclear what is happening to them when they first develop symptoms of a mental health and substance use disorder. By relating your experience, you help others reflect on what they are going through: the confusion, the various explanations for symptoms that they and others came up with, the sense of shame or embarrassment that some people experience, and the ambivalence about taking action. This type of recovery story can help during what often feels like an isolating experience.

2. **Decision(s) to Seek Help.** These decisions are often complex and fairly individual. Explaining how you came to the decision to seek help will help others think about how they are deciding to get help (or not). Your job is not to tell them what they should do, but to help them think clearly and come to a good decision that is *their* decision. Avoid the mistake of telling a story that conveys only the benefits of treatment and not the costs. Stories that mention only the benefits make you sound like a salesperson for treatment and undermine your credibility. A good story about your decisions should free them to talk and think openly and objectively about their own decisions.

3. **The Process of Getting Help.** Taking steps to get help and actually receiving the help we need are not the same thing, and we often face challenges in this transition. A good recovery story can help people anticipate these challenges and be ready to persist when there are delays or diversions in getting the help they really need.

4. **The Treatment Process**. People often try to imagine what clinical help will be like, and their images are often not accurate. Recovery stories that include descriptions of what participating in treatment is like are very helpful in correcting misunderstandings. Your story should include what happens in treatment, how long it takes, what is uncomfortable or unpleasant about it, what is positive or enjoyable about it, and what are the costs involved (money, time, hassle). Be sure to talk about what the providers are like. Many people have a secret fear that providers will judge or shame them in some way. This seems to reflect our own fear of embarrassment, as most clinicians are not at all judgmental. Again, the issue of trust is often at the core of people's concerns about engaging in treatment.

5. **Peer Support and Self-Help.** Similarly, people often have misunderstandings of what it is like to be involved in peer support or self-help groups. They may have tried some type of meeting once or twice and concluded that all groups are like the one they tried. A good recovery story about peer support and self-help groups will again talk about the actual experience: what meetings are like, what is helpful, what is not, and what the people are like. People may think they have to accept everything that a group or organization states. I see this often, for example, with concerns that if someone attends AA, then they have to believe in God. A good recovery story might help them see that they will still have the freedom to take what is helpful in any group and to pass on other elements.

6. **The Recovery Process.** You can describe the entire recovery process from the beginning of the clinical need, to recognition of the need, initial efforts to get help,

experiences in treatment, short-term successes and failures, eventual sustained success, the experience of being in recovery, and lessons learned. People may have difficulty imagining what it will be like to be in recovery. Many may have an unspoken assumption that they can't recover and so can't imagine a happy life on the other side of their illness. Stories about that process, including descriptions of what it is like to have recovered—what you do in your life, what makes you happy, and so on—will be of great value in helping them do the difficult work of starting and sustaining their own recovery.

7. **Taking New Risks.** Participating in self-help groups or treatment is a risk, and we are often hesitant to take risks. Recovery stories that focus on this theme will be very useful. Most situations will call for stories that show the benefits of taking the risk to try to get help. It can be helpful in particular to talk about the experience of taking a risk to get help and having a disappointment—but persisting despite that. This is such a common experience that it is beneficial to ensure that others know they should expect some challenges and that success depends on persisting.

Web-Based Recovery Stories

You are not limited to recovery stories from your life or the lives of people you know. There are growing collections of recovery stories on the web (both written and video) that can be very helpful for the people you serve. These stories represent almost every illness and are told by people from different backgrounds, genders, age, and experiences. Research suggests that people will benefit from hearing stories from someone like them and that those stories will have a more powerful impact. It is easy to discount the recovery story of someone who has not struggled with the same problem, or who is much older/younger than you, or who is different from you in some way. Sometimes this is a valid concern ("Can your experience really be a good model for me?"), and sometimes it is a defense against disappointment ("Sure, a person like you can recover, but not someone like me!"). Consider the following sources for additional recovery stories:

1. **Make the Connection (www.maketheconnection.net).** This website contains a large, well-organized collection of high-quality video and written recovery stories told by veterans. It is organized by problem and by the demographics of the person telling the story. Stories are also organized by whether they focus on recognizing signs and symptoms, the experiences of different illnesses, the experience of different treatments, and other life events and experiences. This website is ideal for working with veterans, but the stories are relevant to others as well.

2. **YouTube Mental Health Recovery Stories.** YouTube has a large collection of videos of people telling recovery stories about different illnesses, different treatment experiences, and different recovery experiences. Unfortunately, it is not well organized, and the quality is uneven. Those affiliated with universities or other large organizations tend to be of better quality. I would suggest getting familiar with these, and then searching for specific topics as the need arises. Be aware that you'll need to vet any videos before using them with clients, as some are poorly designed and include unhelpful information or messaging.

3. **National Alliance on Mental Illness (NAMI) Personal Stories.** NAMI offers a good resource of web-based written recovery stories. Their website (www.NAMI.org/Personal -Stories) contains a directory of

more than four hundred stories covering a wide variety of topics related to illness, help seeking, and recovery. Many of the stories are from family members of people with a mental illness and can be particularly helpful when working with families. Again, I would encourage you to vet any story before sharing it with a client.

PEERS PROVIDE "BRIDGING" TO SERVICES AND SUPPORTS

Research suggests that transitions in healthcare are the most vulnerable spots in the process of recovery. When people are moving into treatment, between services, or out of services, they are particularly vulnerable to falling out of the process. They may relapse. They may stop participating in any care. Part of this is the ambivalence about trying something new, and part of it is the common anxiety about meeting someone new. Peer Support Specialists are very well positioned to help people successfully navigate those transitions by providing a service called "bridging."

Bridging is the process of helping someone transition into a new relationship with a provider, self-help group, or community resource. It involves having contact with and knowledge of the new resource, talking with the client about beginning to work with that resource, personally introducing the client to that resource, possibly accompanying them to meet the new resource, and following up long enough to ensure that the person has successfully made the transition to using that resource. Peers use the trust their clients have in them to help those clients meet and trust new resources and new people. Without that personal touch, the success rate of those transitions can be much lower.

PEERS CAN BE EFFECTIVE ADVOCATES

The role of Peer Support Specialist includes advocacy. Peers encourage people to advocate for themselves but also advocate for clients when it is appropriate. Peers recognize that the world of clinical care and self-help groups includes large numbers of programs and people and that not all options are ideal for each client. It is not uncommon that successful treatment depends on some negotiation between clients and the healthcare system or other people. In those situations, peers often have more knowledge than the client, and the credibility both with the client and the system to help foster those negotiations.

IN SUMMARY

The process of helping clients seek the help they need is fairly complex. Peers are ideally positioned to help in a number of ways, but to do it well, they need to be very aware of what they are doing and the motives and pressures they are feeling. This table may be of help to ensure you navigate these challenges successfully.

Table 1: Peers' Role in Encouraging Help Seeking

Peers Do	Peers Don't
Recognize that recovery is very individual and there are many ways to achieve it. Peers respect the variations in how to recover.	Make assumptions about how people must achieve recovery or assume that others must recover in the same way they did.
Respect the right and responsibility of everyone to make their own decisions about how they recover. This includes decisions about whether to use peer support groups, self-help groups like AA and NA (Narcotics Anonymous), and/or professional healthcare as part of their recovery.	Act as though the peer's opinion or advice about a healthcare decision is more important than the person's right to make their own decision.
Encourage people to use whatever supports or services may be helpful to their recovery.	Encourage people to use only supports or services that the peer is experienced with.
Encourage people to use supports based only on the welfare of the person being served.	Encourage people to enter treatment for reasons other than the welfare of the person served. These could include the financial benefits of the treatment provider or of the peer.

Peers Do	Peers Don't
Provide others with accurate information about resources that could help them recover, including information about self-help groups and professional treatment.	Provide only information on those options the peer supports.
Use strategies to help respectfully persuade people to pursue recovery.	Use strategies to inappropriately or disrespectfully pressure or coerce people to enter treatments they need.
Provide information to people about illness, healthcare services, and recovery in an effort to help them make decisions about entering treatment.	Withhold or distort information about illness, healthcare services, or recovery in order to persuade someone to enter treatment.
Follow up with someone who entered recommended care to see how it worked out.	Fail to follow up, leaving someone who followed the peer's recommendation without any chance to give feedback or to receive follow-up support.
Share their own experience and knowledge that could help someone make a healthcare decision.	Fail to share information that might help clients make informed decisions.
Protect the privacy of people who share their thoughts about their healthcare decisions.	Inappropriately share information about people's decisions with others who do not need to know.

CHAPTER 4

COMMON PATTERNS IN HOW PEOPLE ENTER TREATMENT

The process by which people decide to seek help and then actually get that help is complex and varies depending on the problem, the person, and the setting. There are common patterns that can help us focus our efforts on the key challenges that delay the process. One way to think about this process, as has been described by researchers, is that there are "pathways to care" (Rogler & Cortes, 1993). Here at the core elements of the pathways to care:

1. **Symptoms Appear.** Illnesses are primarily recognizable by the presence of symptoms, and most illnesses usually have patterns, with certain symptoms appearing first. For panic disorder, for example, symptoms typically start in a very abrupt way, with an uncomfortable panic attack. For substance use disorders, the onset is gradual, as the substance use may vary over time with an overall pattern of gradual increase both in use and tolerance. Symptoms

vary in how easy they are to identify. When they start gradually, the person may find it more difficult to recognize that something is wrong. Symptoms that come and go may also be difficult to recognize, as they may not last long enough for the person to decide that something is wrong.

2. **Recognition That Something Is Wrong.** At what point does someone, either the person or a family member or friend, recognize that something is wrong? If we focus first on when the person recognizes the problem, it is clear that it varies widely. Researchers suggest several key factors that predict how long this will take. First, there is the degree to which the person is aware of how they are feeling. Some people do not pay much attention to their own experience, and so the early signs of a problem pass by them with no recognition or concern. Second, people interpret their experience of those symptoms differently. Some may have learned about or experienced mental illness, and so recognize the symptoms fairly easily. Others may not have that experience and/or education, and so interpret the symptoms in inaccurate ways that delay efforts to seek help. I have talked to many people who first interpreted their symptoms in ways that fit with their self-image: "I'm a bad person." "I'm an incompetent person." "I'm a lazy person." Some lived with that interpretation for years before another person helped them see that they were suffering with an illness and that treatment was available. Third, conversations with others often influence how quickly people recognize a problem. Researchers have found a lot of variation in these conversations, with some friends, family, and even providers giving inaccurate interpretations of symptoms that lead to delayed recognition. Cultural norms can be a

key factor here too. In some subcultures, mental health symptoms are interpreted as something other than a mental illness. Stigma around mental illness is common, but the way stigma plays out varies by subgroup.

3. **First Step(s) Taken to Get Help.** Once there is a fairly accurate recognition that there is a problem and that treatment is available to address that problem, the next step is taking action—but what action? Researchers suggest that this step almost always involves other people (friends, family, acquaintances), all serving as potential consultants to guide what to do. Some of these other people are knowledgeable, and some are not. Some have incentives for their relative or friend to avoid entering treatment, and some will have incentives for treatment entry. There is some evidence that particularly tight-knit families are associated with slower movement of any of their members to get mental health treatment.

   Professionals may become involved in giving feedback about the possibility of seeking help. These may include healthcare providers, religious leaders, educators, and so on. These individuals may have their own biases and their own incentives. The first steps after recognition can vary widely depending on the impact of those groups of people.

4. **Finding and Getting the Right Help.** Research suggests that individuals often do not get the help they need in their first contact with healthcare professionals. The professional might not be able to provide the needed treatment. The problem might not be accurately recognized. The care offered may not be what is needed or may not be initially acceptable to the person. The dropout rate after first treatment attempts is estimated to

be between 20 and 60 percent, suggesting that the initial contacts often fail—probably for a variety of reasons. The goal is for every person to get the help they need to successfully recover from the illness they are struggling with. There is plenty of research to document that success is common—but that it often is delayed even when people start the right treatment. In addition to dropping out, failure to follow through with the appropriate treatment is also common. Both dropping out and poor participation are associated with bad outcomes. If we look back at those who have recovered, we can often see that they had some unsuccessful initial attempts to get the right treatment before they were successful. I have asked many patients and providers if they can predict who is ready to participate successfully in treatment, and all say no.

Figure 1: Pathways to Care

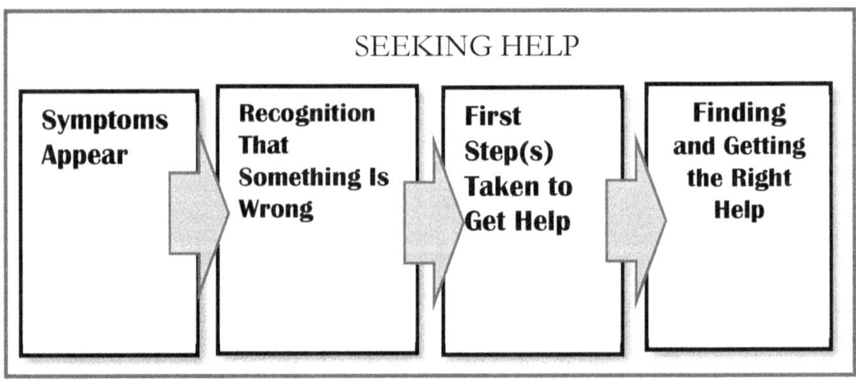

We can see some common patterns in help seeking.

1. **"Rapid" Entry.** Some people move fairly quickly through these "pathways," from recognizing the problem, to taking initial steps to get help, to

participating in the appropriate treatment. Some factors that seem to be common in these situations include:

- The initial symptoms are fairly dramatic and distressing. No one waits for treatment for a broken leg. While mental illnesses are not quite as dramatic or painful as a broken bone, illnesses like panic disorder often have a fairly dramatic start and are very uncomfortable.

- The person is very aware of their experience. Whether it is a personality trait, education, or a cultural factor, some individuals are very aware of their mood, thoughts, and actions, and so they recognize changes in themselves more quickly than others. Efforts to educate the public about the first signs of mental illness have helped speed recognition.

- Knowledge about treatment is associated with more rapid recognition and action. If we don't know that there are solutions, or good solutions, then we have a natural tendency to delay recognition of a problem. Again, efforts to educate the public about treatment options have helped speed recognition and action.

- Access to the appropriate treatment is also a factor. Depending on insurance and finances, some treatments are not available to some people. Knowing that you can participate in a treatment and can afford it makes it easier to take action.

2. **Delayed Entry—Slow Recognition.** In this pattern, the main barrier to help seeking is that the person does not see their symptoms as a clear departure from prior experience. Imagine that a person who has felt depressed much of their life begins to feel more depressed than usual. The increase in symptoms is often hard to recognize. Imagine also that they have very little knowledge of mental health. They don't know what clinical depression is and what the symptoms are, and no one in their family has experience with depression. They may confuse symptoms of depression for other things (e.g., laziness, tiredness, sadness over a loss), and it could take years and years, and the input of other people, before the person thinks, "Maybe this is depression."

3. **Delayed Entry—Slow Action.** In this pattern, the main barrier is not recognition but difficulty taking action. Again, let's consider someone struggling with depression. Possibly they had a family member treated for depression, and so they know the symptoms and the treatments. When they have symptoms, this prior experience or knowledge helps them recognize that they are experiencing depression but doesn't lead to action. Why? They may not want to enter treatment. They may not know where they would go for treatment. They may not want the stigma of being in treatment for a mental illness. They may have a strong desire to solve things for themselves, and so going into treatment might feel like a failure. Maybe the symptoms of depression, which often include apathy and low energy, simply make it hard to take the step of contacting a provider, making an appointment, and showing up for that appointment. Whatever factors contribute to the slowness in action, the result is that the illness continues untreated.

4. **Initial Help Is Sought, Followed by Delay.** In this common pattern, someone has taken action to the point of seeking help from someone—maybe a primary care doctor or religious counselor, maybe even to the point of entering the needed treatment or peer support. A large number of people take these initial steps but then stop and do not participate in the correct treatment or peer support group long enough to get results. The initial treatment or group may not be right. The provider may not be a good match. The group might not be what the person really needs. Something about that initial contact with treatment leads to a delay in the process. First impressions are powerful, and first experiences in treatment often do not result in immediate success. I've met many people who conclude that "treatment doesn't work," "all doctors are rude," "all self-help groups are a waste of time," or some version of these expressions—all based on one visit. A colleague often tells people, "When you were young and you first started dating, if the first date did not go well, you did not give up on marriage, did you? A simple bad match with a support group or a clinician does not mean that all groups and all treatments do not work." Unfortunately, these early conclusions can lead to years of further delay in help seeking.

5. **No Entry.** Depending on the situation and the illness, some people never enter treatment. I worked with a man in his sixties whose parents were then in their eighties. Both parents had been heavy daily alcohol users for his entire life, and both were dependent on alcohol and could not stop without withdrawal. Unfortunately, both drank over their entire adulthood and never acknowledged that they had a problem despite the efforts of their children and friends. Both eventually died, never having participated in any treatment. As you can imagine,

it took a great deal of effort on their part to avoid getting help. They were able to work most of their adult life. Their physical health had not deteriorated, as is the case for many with an alcohol use disorder, and so while their primary care doctor repeatedly recommended they stop drinking, they were still healthy enough to ignore her recommendations. But their symptoms had a cost. They had very strained relationships with their children and neighbors and a history of troubles at work. Both had withdrawn from family and friends, doctors, and religious organizations, all in an effort to avoid others seeing their drinking. But the costs were not abrupt or severe enough to persuade them to seek help.

SPECIAL SITUATION: Involuntary and Leveraged Treatment

In this situation, people enter treatment against their own will. In general, state and federal laws protect people's right to choose whether they will participate in any type of healthcare, including mental health services. There are some rare exceptions. If the person is a danger to themselves or others, *involuntary* hospitalization is possible. In some settings, forced treatments can be legal when a clear and dramatic need is present. Hospitalization typically leads to some treatment benefit, and that often leads to outpatient care, which also can help. While this is clearly not an ideal way to enter any treatment, for some it is the beginning of steps that do lead to voluntary treatment and eventual recovery.

A related path to getting needed help involves "leveraged" treatment. In these situations, the individual with symptoms is resistant to entering care but is facing another outcome that they like even less than treatment (Monahan et al., 2005). A common example is someone who was arrested for an offense related to their mental illness and/or substance use disorder. Increasingly, judges and specialty courts will try to use the potential consequences of jail to influence the person to enter needed treatment. This may be in the context of a "drug court," "mental health court," or "veterans court." Research on these legal tools indicates they typically result in positive outcomes for participants (Hartley & Baldwin, 2019; Honegger, 2015).

Similarly, social service programs and benefits have been used to encourage people to overcome ambivalence about treatment. Housing programs typically have rules that can encourage or require treatment when someone's untreated mental illness results in behavior that can lead to discharge from the program. Other people receive financial benefits that are managed by a professional or a family member. It is not uncommon that conditions, including participation in treatment, are placed on the person if they are to receive their own funds.

Even less formally, but no less common, family members and friends can place requirements on an individual with an untreated mental illness that they need to enter treatment in order to avoid a negative outcome (Grzywacz & Fuqua, 2000). I've met many people who entered treatment because their spouse or partner threatened to leave them if they did not.

"Leveraged" decisions range from mild social pressure to manipulative and coercive arrangements. There can be clearly abusive situations that inappropriately override a person's freedom of choice. There can also be valuable and logical decisions that help a person make a healthy decision to seek needed help. For advocates, it can be difficult to see these options clearly. I have met Peer Support Specialists who view any effort to leverage treatment engagement as coercive, violating the freedom of the person who does not want to seek help. While I appreciate the value of freedom in decision-making, it is not helpful to overly simplify how we see these situations. Virtually all our decisions have external factors that "leverage" or pressure us one way or another. If we are to be effective in helping our clients, we have to be aware of the potential for both abusive and helpful leveraging by others in their lives.

Figure 2: The Cascading Effects of Untreated Illness

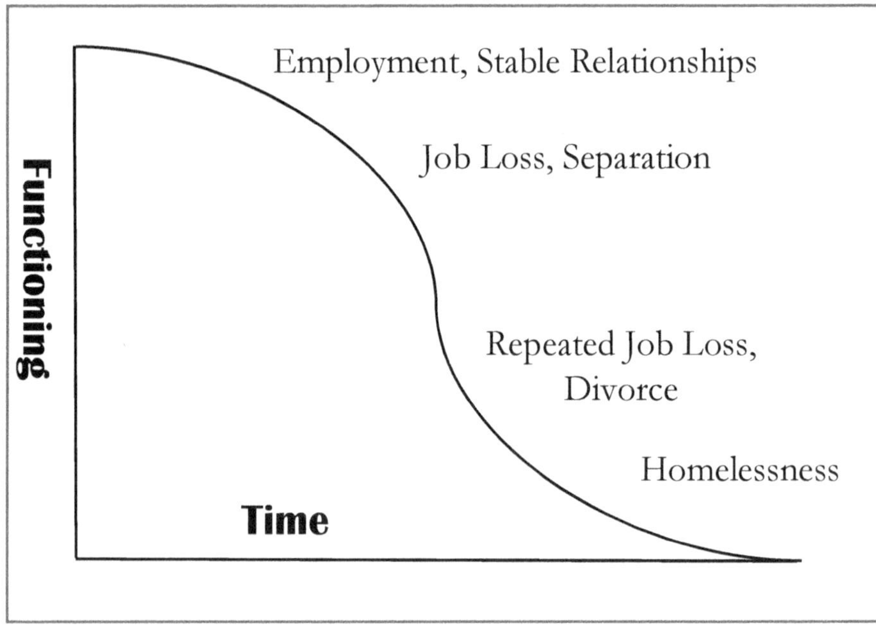

THE COMMON IMPACT OF DELAYED CARE

While delays in getting help are common, they are typically very costly to the person, their family, their employer, the larger community, and often the healthcare industry. Untreated symptoms often represent unnecessary suffering. More concerning, those symptoms often lead to declines in functioning, such as difficulties at work or school, difficulties in relating to friends and family, and eventually difficulties in maintaining the basic elements of a healthy lifestyle—self-care, housing, and so on. Figure 2 represents the broad pattern of the impact of untreated symptoms on functioning over time. Small functional problems create more symptoms and more functional problems, as the consequences of delayed treatment cascade toward greater and greater loss. The length of time and the speed of decline will be very different depending on the person, the symptoms, and a host of other factors, but the overall pattern underlines the importance of helping people make good decisions about seeking help early.

CHAPTER 5

UNDERSTANDING PEOPLE'S AMBIVALENCE

Ambivalence is defined as the coexistence within an individual of positive and negative feelings toward something, such as a person or an action, simultaneously drawing the person in opposite directions. An example of ambivalence could be a person who feels that they want to apply for a job promotion because of the higher pay but they simultaneously do not want to apply because of fear that they may fail. Ambivalence is a psychological state that can influence behavior but is separate from it. You may choose to apply or not apply for that job, but you may still feel ambivalent.

Ambivalence is extremely common—we all feel it about many things. We are commonly ambivalent both about things we chose not to do and things we chose to do. We are often ambivalent about things that we most publicly support or deny. For example, it is common that people have mixed feelings about the people they love most intensely. They also may feel some attraction to things that they hate the most.

Awareness of ambivalence is key to understanding people's decisions about seeking help and participating in clinical care or peer support groups. I assume that everyone has mixed feelings about getting professional help, including those who seek it and those who do not. For Peer Support Specialists the right question is not whether someone feels ambivalent about getting help, but what feelings make up that ambivalence and how the people we serve can make good decisions in a situation in which they are ambivalent.

In chapter 11 we will look closely at a set of tools from motivational interviewing. One of these tools is described as a "motivational matrix" and helps people clarify their ambivalence about any decision. It is a simple two-by-two table, with the two columns representing "Making the Change" and "Not Changing," while the two rows represent "Costs and Lost Opportunities" and "Benefits." Table 2 represents a motivational matrix someone might fill out as they think about whether they should start attending a self-help group for weight loss. Each motivational matrix will reflect the person and the problem.

Table 2: Hypothetical Motivational Matrix for Client Considering Self-Help Groups for Weight-Loss

	Seeking Help	**Not Seeking Help**
Costs and Lost Opportunities	"I'll feel embarrassed to be there" 2 hours per week of my time to attend meetings	Continue to be overweight Continued depression Continued feelings of isolation
Benefits	I will feel less alone Possible new friends who relate to being overweight Potential to recover functioning Easy access to new social support	No risk to feel better No need to acknowledge that there is a problem Don't have to meet new people – I have social anxiety

If we think about the decision to enter a needed healthcare service, we see some common patterns across the motivational matrix.

People often do not carefully think through decisions to seek help, and specifically do not consider the costs and benefits of all their options. For example, they may focus on one cost of seeking help and ignore the benefits. Poor understanding of all the relevant costs and benefits often contributes to confusion and poor decisions. Research suggests that better understanding of all the factors leads to better decisions (Miller & Rose, 2015).

THINKING ABOUT HOW PEOPLE MAKE CHANGES: THE STAGES OF CHANGE MODEL

In 1986, two scientists studying people in the process of recovery from substance use disorders developed the "transtheoretical" model of change, which provides a simple way to understand and influence the change process (Prochazka & DiClemente, 1986). Further research has found that the model may not always fit people's experience, but I find it a useful tool to think about the people we serve. The model assumes that change can follow a wide variety of patterns but that there are common stages in the process and that each stage creates opportunities for others to support the change. The stages include:

Precontemplation. This stage is characterized by no intention to change in the foreseeable future. The person may be unaware that there is a problem at all, or may be only partially aware of it. They often have other explanations for what is happening and so do not think any action on their part is required. Sometimes people in the precontemplation stage end up in contact with Peer Support Specialists, and some may even end up entering treatment. When this happens, it is usually because some external person or process forced them into treatment. The concern is that, without recognition on the person's part, it is unlikely they will really engage meaningfully in treatment, and so may be wasting their own and others' time and energy.

Contemplation. People in the contemplation stage are aware that a problem exists and are thinking seriously about making a change to address it. They have not made a commitment to change anything, which is why this stage focuses on contemplation. At this stage people may be struggling to decide between the benefits of making a change and the benefits of staying the same. People can get stuck in this stage, which can take a long time to resolve.

Action. People who have entered the action stage have made a commitment to change, and so are taking steps to change their behavior or environment in order to address the problem. Examples include talking to their primary care provider, asking advice from friends or Peer Support Specialists, and starting to attend a support group or clinical treatment. Because changes are happening, some people think that this is the entire change process, missing the importance of the earlier and later stages. Active efforts to change usually occur in a time-limited period, often happening in less than six months.

Maintenance. People in the maintenance stage have made a change and now are actively seeking to maintain that change. The work needed to maintain a change is often different from that needed to start the change. For some conditions, including those often described as "relapsing" or "remitting" illnesses, such as substance dependence, psychosis, bipolar disorder, and some forms of depression, periods of maintenance can be interrupted by relapses, which then may lead to another cycle of contemplation, action, and maintenance.

How Can We Help a Person in the Precontemplation Stage?

In this stage, people benefit the most from conversations that lead to increased awareness of themselves, their problem, and their defenses against dealing with the problem. As they are not even thinking about making a change, efforts to push a change often lead to greater resistance. However, they may benefit from a greater awareness of the costs of the behavior and how it is affecting them and their relationships. Peer Support Specialists often have particularly valuable real-life information and credibility to help others consider these issues, and move to the contemplation stage.

How Can We Help a Person in the Contemplation Stage?

People in this stage are attempting to think through whether a change is needed and, if so, how to make it. They are seeking to make the change themselves, so efforts to push them can again result in unfortunate resistance to change. Conversations that add to their knowledge about the problem, the treatment, and the recovery process can be very helpful at this point, as they will increase the information needed for a good decision. Here, a discussion of the motivational matrix can be of help to them in clarifying some of the possible benefits of change and costs they are paying for their current situation. Recovery stories may also be particularly valuable in helping people understand decisions to make a change.

How Can We Help a Person in the Action Stage?

At this stage the person is making changes and watching to see what benefits and problems arise from those changes. They often benefit from encouragement from others and the natural rewards that result from solving the problem. Conversations in which those benefits are highlighted, or in which their change efforts are supported, will encourage them to persist. People often struggle with confidence at this point, fearing that they cannot sustain the changes. Peer Support Specialists again have a key role here, emphasizing the person's ability to make the change and sharing personal experiences of taking action with positive results.

How Can We Help a Person in the Maintenance Stage?

In this stage, less energy is being expended to change, as the change is in place and must be maintained. People in the maintenance stage often benefit from peer support and help networking into more positive social networks that will further support the change. They will also benefit from conversations about maintenance strategies and how to respond to relapses. It may help to remind them that relapses are not uncommon and are part of the recovery process. It may also be helpful at this point to talk about the challenges of getting used to being in recovery. For some people, recovery will be a fairly new experience and may feel uncomfortable. At this stage, peers and peer support groups play a key role in modeling and encouraging stable recovery.

As mentioned, subsequent research has shown that this model of change may be more of a useful guide than an accurate description of how everyone changes. It appears clear that these stages are not always mutually exclusive (Littell & Girvin, 2002; Quadri, Kanji, Naing & Huqh, 2021) **and that people don't** always move through them in the same order. I include the model here because it can be a useful way to think about where someone is in the process of changing at any one moment and what kind of support you can provide to encourage positive movement.

CHAPTER 6

FOCUSING IN ON THE MOST COMMON BARRIERS

To be effective in helping people recover, we need to know the most common barriers they face to seeking needed help.

INTERNAL BARRIERS

Self-Reliance. Self-reliance and independence are good traditional American values—values that we see in our cultural images and that are particularly encouraged in some key subgroups, including military personnel and those living in rural areas. *Self-reliance* is defined as the "reliance upon one's own powers and resources rather than those of others." When it applies to healthcare, it usually refers to the tendency of people to want to rely upon their own resources to deal with symptoms or functional challenges instead of reaching out for the help of other people or clinical providers. Self-reliance is consistently found to be related to reduced help seeking for mental health conditions (Jennings et al., 2015; Holdsambeck, 2021). It is the most common reason given for not seeking help by people living in rural areas (Fischer et al., 2016).

While self-reliance is a positive value, there is flaw in the self-sufficient stance when it comes to recovery. No one is completely self-sufficient. We rely on others to help us meet our varied needs for food, shelter, safety, and so on, just as they rely on us. That is the basic agreement of any community. No one considers it a failure of self-reliance if we go to the store to buy our food or allow a teacher to educate our children. Healthcare is the same. Is it a failure to seek the help of doctors to deal with a medical emergency? Why is it a failure to need the help of providers to deal with other medical issues like depression or substance use? It is not, but many people react as though it is.

Self-reliance may be a way to simply avoid taking action. Researchers asked people in the community about whether they would seek help if they had a mental health condition; many indicated they would not, saying, "I want to take care of it myself" (Sareen et al., 2007). In a survey of people who tried to commit suicide, only 50 percent took any action to get help in the following year. When researchers asked the 50 percent who did not seek out help why they didn't, many said, "I want to take care of it myself" (Bruffaerts et al., 2011). Is this actual self-reliance or simple denial? It ultimately doesn't matter, as we still need to address the stated preference for self-reliance.

To address inappropriate "self-reliance," you want to listen for the flawed logic of extreme self-reliance and help others see the ways it gets us into trouble.

1. Raise questions about whether it is practically helpful in that situation to not ask for help. What is the outcome in reality, and is that what they want for themselves and others?

2. Contrast their value of "self-reliance" with the values of *wisdom* in taking care of problems so that we can move on in life, *service* and *love* to take care of problems for the sake of ourselves and others, and *courage* to face new challenges.

3. Emphasize how even the most self-reliant people still need others to help. They provide assistance to neighbors and they receive help as well. We all work together, and asking for help is just part of being in a community.

4. Raise questions about the long-term impact of extreme self-reliance. "What will happen to you and your loved ones over time if you keep avoiding seeking needed help? How is that good for you or for them? How does that fit with your love for them?"

Stoicism. Stoicism is related to self-reliance, but there are some important differences. While the term can refer to a school of philosophy, when the term *stoicism* is used to describe people's behavior, it is usually referring to the tendency to patiently endure pain or problems without expressing unhappiness, with an emphasis on self-control and not showing "weakness." This approach values personal strength, patience, and courage, which are positive. Like self-reliance, there is a flaw in stoicism when it is taken too far. Is it appropriate to endure suffering when it is possible to reduce or even eliminate that suffering? Someone who won't see a doctor for intense chest pain is experiencing needless risk and suffering, and creating bigger problems for themselves and other people. That type of needless suffering is not a sign of strength or courage but rather of poor judgment and lack of concern for self and others. To be appropriately caring and responsible to oneself and others requires that we analyze problems, and when the problem is solvable, we take action to solve it. To help others overcome misguided stoicism:

1. First, help them talk about why they are not taking action and then emphasize the values of *responsibility* to self and others, and the *courage* it takes to ask for help.

2. Distinguish necessary suffering from unnecessary suffering. If we can solve a problem, the suffering that results from avoiding efforts to resolve it is unnecessary.

3. In some cases, it can be helpful to point out that they have seen other people play the "martyr" role and that this role is not helpful. This is a commonly used term for people who suffer needlessly in order to gain something from other people. Simply mentioning this term can help some people recognize that they are suffering needlessly.

Fear. Fear is one of our most powerful motivators and is often behind other stated reasons for not seeking help. Fear is tied to survival and so has great value in some situations. For that reason, the brain has a strong network to support fear, and it tends to take work to manage a specific fear once it is in place. It is not uncommon for people to have fears, even extreme fears, that are irrational. These get going and are sustained by those brain systems that are designed to keep us safe, even when we are not really at risk.

Fear focuses on risk as opposed to benefit, and so in general, fear encourages us to avoid situations that result in risk. For that reason, fear is not a great motivator for change; instead, it tends to encourage us to avoid change. In healthcare decisions, we are often facing the fear of *the possibility* of a negative outcome. "What could happen if I reach out for help? What could happen if I try to change my life?" There are real risks in healthcare. But fear often exaggerates those risks or focuses on them without considering the costs of not taking action to change. To help others address inappropriate fear about seeking help:

1. Help them talk about what they are afraid of. Their comments will often help them understand what is behind their decisions and will make it easier for you and them to see the flaws in those fears.

2. Raise questions about what the real risk is as opposed to the feeling of risk. Is a bad outcome likely? What do they base their fear on—accurate information or a story from a single person or a single experience?

3. Help them see the cost of not taking action. The bad outcomes that are common for those who avoid seeking help are something to fear as well. They tend to grow and become more complicated over time. Help balance their fear of taking action with the fear of what happens when you don't. Chapters 17–24 provide you with specific data about the risks and costs of not seeking help for common mental illnesses.

4. Emphasize the value of courage and its role in solving problems. Recovery stories about courage are a common tool for helping people see that recovery often depends on moments when courageous decisions lead to big changes for the good. Remind them that courage does not mean lack of fear but taking action in the face of fear.

Low Self-Efficacy. The psychologist Albert Bandura defined the term *self-efficacy* as one's belief in one's ability to succeed in accomplishing a task (Bandura, 2000). The term is roughly equivalent to confidence. For our purposes, we will focus on confidence to complete three related tasks: seeking help, participating in treatment, and recovering from an illness. Lack of confidence that we can do any of these can lead us to avoid efforts to seek help. This makes sense, as why should we try to seek help if we don't believe we can do it effectively or that we can be successful once we get the help?

Many mental illnesses fit a pattern called "relapsing and remitting." This means that they get better and then get worse, often without any real explanation. Many people with depression or substance use disorders will experience periods when their symptoms will get better followed later by times when they will get worse. Many people will achieve recovery for a period of time, only to relapse and have to reestablish a new period of recovery. This pattern is common in other medical illnesses as well, including diabetes, multiple sclerosis, rheumatoid arthritis, and lupus. Unfortunately, when people relapse in a mental health condition, it is not uncommon for them to blame themselves—to see it as a personal failure. That is why self-efficacy can be low in people who've experienced even one relapse, or who have seen others relapse.

For some people, their lack of self-efficacy will be specific to those tasks. They are confident that they can do other things effectively, but they don't believe they can get help or recover. In many cases, that belief is based on past experiences in which they tried and failed, or saw other people try and fail. For others, their lack of self-efficacy is more general—they have no confidence that they can succeed at anything.

To help people with low self-efficacy seek the help they need, you may want to consider the following:
1. First distinguish whether they have low confidence in their ability to do most things or whether it is specific to seeking help and recovery. Your actions will be different depending on which group they are in.

2. If they have low self-efficacy focused on seeking help and/or recovering, you want to help them examine what they base that on. Is this based on their own experience, the difficulties they have seen in other people, or stories they have heard about others? Self-efficacy is an estimate based on information, and you can help change their confidence by providing better information about what happens when people seek help and recover.

3. If their low confidence is based on their experience of relapse, you may want to help them understand relapse better. Most **people don't understand that,** by nature, many mental illnesses are relapsing-remitting disorders. Relapses should be reframed as something that can be expected, not that recovery is impossible.

4. If they have low self-efficacy about most things—not just recovery—you will want to help them see that. This is a broader issue, but the solution can involve similar steps. Do not try to address their overall confidence, but start to challenge their assumptions about their confidence in their ability to recover.

5. You may want to be prepared with different types of information that different people may need. Recovery stories about seeking help, participating in treatment, and recovering are convincing to some people and will go a long way to improve their self-efficacy. For others, you will want to have some more general scientific data about the success rates of people recovering with different illnesses. Chapters 17–24 include information you can use about success rates for common treatments and about long-term recovery rates.

6. Listen for the "anecdotal bias." We tend to be persuaded by stories of people's experience when we don't know a lot about the bigger picture. The recovery rate for depression is very good, but if we don't know that and we talk to someone who tells us a compelling story of how they have failed at overcoming depression, we may conclude that recovery from depression is very rare. Similarly, we may hear from someone who tried to go to AA or NA and failed, and conclude that no one gets help from "those groups," when scientific data shows that many people benefit. Listen for what people are basing their conclusions on, and be ready to challenge the "anecdotal bias" when you hear it.

7. You may want to introduce them to people who have been successful at the task they have low confidence that they can do. If they lack confidence that they can work with a psychotherapist, for example, introduce them to a Peer Support Specialist who worked well with a psychotherapist and who can talk openly about what that was like. If they have had multiple relapses and so have no confidence they can recover over time, introduce them to a peer who had similar experiences and then has sustained recovery. You can actually use the "anecdotal bias" by helping people meet real-life successes.

Misunderstanding of Illness and Treatment. Health and healthcare are highly complex areas in which our brightest doctors no longer understand portions of medicine and have to focus on specialized areas if they want to fully understand all the knowledge about one area. Medical knowledge is currently doubling every five years, meaning that the average patient has no hope of knowing everything they need to know about the illnesses and treatments they are likely to encounter in their lives.

It is very common and predictable for our clients to have misunderstandings of their illness, the treatments they may participate in, and the outcomes that they can expect. It is unreasonable to expect they would have accurate up-to-date information. The problem is that when people feel that they don't know important information related to a decision they have to make, they tend to be conservative in their decision. They may decide to wait until they feel they know more or to stay with what they have, not risking a change when they know that they don't have all the information. So how do we help in this situation?

To help people who feel they don't have enough information about their illness or treatment, you may want to consider the following strategies:

1. Provide information. Your experience as a peer will lead you to gain more and more knowledge about mental health conditions and treatments. Take advantage of every opportunity to learn and stay curious about your field, as your clients will benefit from your knowledge. Be sure to keep up to date in your own knowledge—it does not take long to fall behind in the new developments, putting you at risk for sharing outdated information. Again, chapters 17–24 are designed to give you some of that information.

2. Help them find resources with up-to-date information. While you can't know everything, you should be able to point clients in the direction of common sources of current trustworthy information. Increasingly these are websites, run by healthcare organizations with reputations for being authorities in the most current information. These would include:

- National Institutes of Health (www.nih.gov/about-nih/what-we-do/nih-turning-discovery-into-health)

- World Health Organization (www.WHO.int)

- Centers for Disease Control and Prevention (CDC)(www.cdc.gov)

- Substance Abuse and Mental Health Services Administration (SAMSHA)(www.samhsa.gov)

- Mayo Clinic (www.mayoclinic.org)

- Johns Hopkins Medicine (www.hopkinsmedicine.org/health)

- Harvard Medical School (www.health.harvard.edu)

- WebMD (www.WebMD.com)

3. Help them gain confidence that what they know represents what authorities in the field know. Focus on their confidence level. The feeling that they **don't know** what they need to know can be a barrier to taking action. If there are unanswered questions that are beyond what the healthcare field knows, they need to know that too. **Don't communicate** falsely that they know everything they need to know. The goal is to know the available information about illnesses and treatments and to make a good decision about care based on that available knowledge.

4. Help them recognize the risks of delaying decisions. We often feel the risk of taking action but are less attentive to the risk of not doing so. You may want to develop some recovery stories from your own life about this topic or refer them to colleagues who can talk about personal experiences with the negative side of not taking action and delaying decisions. Appendix B provides some useful quotes you can use about the risks of not taking action.

5. Connect them with others who have made similar decisions with the available information, such as Peer Support Specialists and other people who can talk about their decisions.

Stigma and Self-Stigma. The psychologist Patrick Corrigan (2015) defines *public stigma*, what we usually refer to simply as *stigma*, as "the prejudice and discrimination directed at a group by the population," and includes "the negative attitudes held by members of the public about people with devalued characteristics." In contrast, he defines *self-stigma* as "what occurs when people internalize negative public attitudes." Self-stigma starts with simple awareness of negative views held by others (family, friends, people in the media, etc.) and creates danger as the person starts to agree with those views, and then apply those views to themselves in a way that reduces their life. For example, some members in the community do not understand mental illness and so may communicate the view that people with mental illness are scary. People with a mental illness may pick up this message through subtle communications in the media and start to feel that they are scary because they have been diagnosed with a mental illness, or avoid entering treatment for fear of being diagnosed and becoming "scary."

Stigma is most destructive when it is unrecognized. As a Peer Support Specialist, one of your key roles is to identify and fight stigma in every setting, regardless of whether it is public stigma or self-stigma. Your clients may not know the concept and may not see it. Be active in educating them about the destructive nature of stigma and gain their involvement in fighting it in their environment and in their own mind.

EXTERNAL BARRIERS

Cost—Money and Time. The costs of getting help are difficult to calculate for any individual. Differences in insurance coverage, regional costs, treatment costs, and differences in ability to afford these costs make this a challenge to understand. Unfortunately, in community surveys, the cost of care is identified as a key barrier that keeps people from seeking care, with particularly high concerns in the US relative to countries with national healthcare systems (Sareen et al., 2007). To help clients address the barrier of cost, consider the following:

1. Outreach workers and Peer Support Specialists usually have limited options to address either the financial or time costs of participating in treatment. Many people will not know the real costs and so are afraid of costs that are higher than is realistic. Helping them track down the specific costs can be very helpful.

2. You can also help people view the costs in light of the benefits of treatment. The motivational matrix (page 101) is a useful tool for understanding costs, as they are only relevant in contrast to the benefits.

3. You may be able to research any support resources available at your organization. Are there special funds to help clients in need? Are there treatment options that reduce the cost of the treatment, either in terms of time or money?

Other Pragmatic Concerns. There are other practical aspects to treatment that influence decisions to seek help. For some people, transportation is a major challenge, and regular treatment requires a great deal of work and expense to arrange for transportation. This can be often overlooked by providers. Sometimes treatment involves specific tasks that are difficult for some clients, such as reading, public speaking, homework, and so on. If we ignore these often-hidden concerns, we will misunderstand why some people choose to avoid treatment.

To address these concerns, I try to always ask about transportation specifically, and any "other concerns" they may have about treatment. Again, you should research any transportation resources that may be helpful at your organization. You may also be able to work as an advocate with providers to address some of the pragmatic concerns, such as reducing the reading or homework, or finding help to address these when necessary.

Family. While most family members will support and even urge people to get help, there are some situations in which family members become a barrier. In surveys, some people in recovery have reported that their family members have discouraged them from getting help to move their recovery forward. That may be hard to imagine, but consider this example:

Winston is a forty-two-year-old unemployed single heterosexual white man with a long history of struggling with schizophrenia. He has been in the hospital fourteen times during his lifetime and has been doing relatively well in the past three years, being in the hospital only once and only for three days. He is starting to feel confident that he can recover and has been a regular attender at the local NAMI support group. He has seen others in that group who are working and wants to talk with you about whether he should consider going to work. He has worked in the past in construction and did fairly well. He really wants to start making money again and contributing to his family's finances. You encourage him, and he starts to work with vocational rehabilitation. He then approaches you to talk with his family about his desire to work, saying, "They are not listening to me. Can you talk with them?"

In preparing to meet with them, you want to anticipate why they may not want to see him return to work. What reasons can you think of?

After talking with them, you realize they have a number of serious concerns:

1. The family states that Winston's original psychiatrist told them that he would "never be able to work again" because of his schizophrenia. They have given up hope that he could work and so are not expecting him to do so. They don't want to be disappointed again.

2. They are concerned that work might cause stress that will result in Winston relapsing again. This has happened in the past when he started to get paranoid about his pay, and then he ended up in this hospital. They say, "He is doing so well now; we would hate to see him get sick again."

3. In the past, Winston has gotten hurt on the job. With his current illness, they ask whether he could do his job safely. Could he get there safely? Wouldn't there be a lot of problems and worries created by him returning to work?

4. Winston currently receives disability income from social security. If he gets a job, he will likely lose that income. The family is concerned that if he has a relapse and loses

his job, then he would have no income, and the family finances need something in the form of income from him.

These four concerns represent four common reasons that family members can be hesitant to support steps toward recovery. They are not unreasonable concerns, and we need to understand and appreciate them before we jump too quickly to answer them. Let's talk through each:

The first concern is really about hope. Whether or not there was a clinician who voiced the idea that the family should not hope for recovery, the family members are very likely to have thought this at one point or another. We all struggle with hope, and they may have lost their hope years before.

You have experience in addressing the core issue of hope with your clients. You should be able to talk about how many people do recover and that many take steps in their recovery like going back to work successfully. You can point out that there are still some clinicians who say things like that, but that most do not feel that way and that researchers have convincing data that most people can go back to work and work successfully.

The family is worried that returning to work (or any other next step in recovery) could create stress that would lead to relapse. Recovery does include challenges, and those challenges can be stressful. It is realistic to worry about relapse and to fear the loss of valuable progress. The cost of a relapse may be paid by the family members, so they may be particularly concerned about it.

Be careful not to try to convince them that there won't be a relapse—there may well be one. The challenge is really in the family's image of how recovery works. They need to understand that relapses are part of recovery, as the person moves forward.

Sometimes there are setbacks, but for most people those are offset by continued improvement. Again, your recovery story and those of other Peer Support Specialists can help them see that relapse is just a part of the picture, and should not block efforts toward work or family or whatever the person wants to pursue.

The family is also concerned about the pragmatic problems that could be caused by this change. Could there be safety risks? What new challenges will be created by the change? Again, this is a realistic concern.

You will want to acknowledge and accept the reality that these pragmatic problems are likely to arise. The issue is, again, one of hope. They may have to help solve these problems, but if it is in the service of the person recovering their life, then that is a great benefit for the cost.

The last concern related to disability income looks like it is only about money, but it includes more than just money. Money in itself is a serious barrier. If the family thinks that recovery risks their financial stability, you will often see very active (and reasonable) resistance. Your knowledge about financial issues and supports can help you here. For example, social security disability income has some protections to ensure that people can transition to work with minimal risk of losing that income in the short-term. That program wants to encourage people to return to work, **and so they've adapted their rules** so this does not become a barrier. The Veterans Health Administration has even stronger protections. You may need to educate the family about this.

Under their concern about money is worry about change. Families often have to reorganize to address the changes caused by a family **member's mental illness**. By recovering, the person is pushing for the family to reorganize again. Some family members may not want to change back. Some may fear that change will not stick and so they may lose what they currently have. There is also a broad tendency for people to want to keep doing what they are doing and to fear change.

Friends, Neighbors, and Work Associates. These individuals can also discourage help seeking. Their concerns often parallel those of the family members. In their concern for their friend, they worry that help seeking could result in negative outcomes. They may remember times when their friend was very symptomatic and how much they suffered. Anything that might cause their friend to go backward would be seen as a very serious risk. Unfortunately, they may not understand the benefits of seeking help.

Other Providers. Like friends and family, other clinical providers can also be barriers to help seeking and/or change. They may have a history with their client that makes them concerned about relapse. They may not have experience with needed treatments or may not have the necessary knowledge about these treatments. They can be a very powerful voice in their client's life, and the recommendation to not seek help can have a very negative impact. For this reason, I always consider how to communicate with other providers to ensure I can provide any needed information and that I understand their view on the situation.

CHAPTER 7

THINKING MORE ABOUT KEY INCENTIVES

Why focus on the benefits of entering treatment? We've talked about the costs of taking action and getting help, but the rewards are usually less often talked about. People need a reason to pay the costs of changing. If they can't come up with a 'why' for taking these steps, they are not likely to act. Often these rewards can be hard for people to visualize.

Many illnesses have been present for years, and so it is difficult to remember a time before. I often ask people if they have recent experience in feeling better, or recent successes, and what those experiences were like. Many people have not, so we need to help them think about what it would be like.

Many benefits are difficult to imagine. What would life be like if they felt less depressed or less anxious? Their image of what change will look like is critical to whether they will seek help. If they cannot imagine it, we need to help them find those images. Again, recovery stories come into play here. Can your stories or those of others in recovery help them imagine what their recovery would be like, and thus give them a reason to take those chances?

Even if they have a clear, tangible goal, there is the issue of confidence. Mental health symptoms and experiences often undermine confidence in specific things (e.g., working or dating successfully) and in broader ways (e.g., "I feel I can't do anything right!"). After asking about people's goals, I always ask them to rate their confidence that they can achieve them. A wonderful goal that I have no confidence that I can achieve is not going to motivate me to change.

As an outreach worker or Peer Support Specialist, you have two goals: (1) help make the rewards clear and (2) build confidence that they can be obtained. But what type of rewards are we talking about?

Reduction or Elimination of Symptoms. This is the area that most people will think about first. They will imagine not feeling depressed or anxious or suicidal. Again, this can be hard to imagine for some. Many symptoms are subtle—we talked about how the research shows that panic attacks are so uncomfortable that people seek help relatively quickly, while depression is more subtle and so people are slower to get help.

One strategy is helping people think about their symptoms and contrast them with how they've felt when they were feeling better or how people without those symptoms feel. Build the contrast in order to make the difference more obvious. People can often visualize an image of freedom from depression or anxiety by thinking of other friends or family, or characters in film or on TV. Those images can be helpful, as they can point out the subtleties of recovery.

Another strategy is to point out that people can get used to their symptoms and erroneously accept them as just part of life. This is most common when the symptoms are subtle, when they've been present for a long time, and for some symptoms that seem to change the way you see life. For example, some people with PTSD start to think that their fears are actually justified, that there is great danger. Again, we need to help them see the contrast between what the symptoms are telling them and what people without the symptoms feel.

For many people, others in their lives can see the symptoms more clearly than they can and make comments that are concerning to the person. "I'm worried that you are depressed." "I think you should talk about this with your doctor." This aspect of having a mental illness can be the most motivating: people don't like others to be concerned, to make those comments, or to take steps to help. I always ask about how others in their life feel about these symptoms and what that is like for them. I've had clients who felt comfortable with their depression or anxiety but who sought help to stop others from worrying. That may not be the ideal motivation, but if it results in someone asking for help, it may be what leads to recovery.

Ability to Do Things - Functioning. While the elimination of symptoms may be the first benefit people think of, it is often not enough to motivate change. People are also asking, "What do I want to feel better *for*?" What do they want in their life that recovery will lead to? This focus often emerges over time, as symptoms limit functioning and people become unhappy with those losses in functioning. They often can be identified in relationships, work, or school (e.g., poorer relationships, lost jobs, trouble performing in school). The impact can be subtle early on but typically becomes more pronounced over time. Trouble attending work on time turns into disciplinary action, and then suspension, and then getting fired. Look for the progression of functional problems and help your clients see these. Help them track the losses back to the early, more subtle problems, and help them see the links with their untreated illness. You may have to help them deal with long-standing denial, as they have been protecting themselves from seeing the costs to their lives. But this will help them make better sense of their experience.

Help your clients refocus from what they have lost in terms of functioning to what they can gain by recovering. If they have lost or damaged relationships, what will those relationships be like when they are repaired? If they have lost jobs, what will it be like to work successfully again? I have found that people often have an image of themselves as a success—something specific, positive, concrete, and attainable. It may be old and they may not believe they can attain it at this point, but it is often valuable to help them talk about it. What was their "dream" for their life? What did they want it to be? Get them talking about it, and then help them think about what parts could be reconstructed through recovery. Creating a clear and compelling image will have a big impact on their willingness to work for it.

Ability to Do Things for Others. Our ability to work or go to school is most motivating when we consider whom we are doing this for. We are often most motivated to do things for others, and particularly for those we love. I have worked with many people who will not work particularly hard for themselves but when it is clear that the work is in the service of their family or friends, they will take great risks and work long and hard.

Whom we want to function for is often under the surface, and we need to ask and then listen to help people identify these key motives. Are there children or grandchildren who need them? Is there a partner or a close friend whom they want to support? Do they want to be someone who contributes to their family or their community? We all need to recover for ourselves, but we often are also recovering so that we can contribute to those we love. Be aware that the "who" may be someone in the future—we may want to work so that we can get a girlfriend/boyfriend who we can care about, to have children, and so on.

Symbolic Rewards. Functional goals like returning to work or graduating from school are often important as symbols of recovery. Sometimes the symbol is more important than the practical value of the activity. I have worked with adults who have pursued recovery over years in a symbolic effort to prove something to themselves or to others. You'll want to listen for this and help them articulate it. They may want to show that "I'm taking care of myself" or "I am an adult—I can be independent of my parents." Others may want to prove someone wrong— prove that those who said they were "hopeless" were not right. Finally, others may frame their recovery in spiritual terms, wanting to recover so that they can live in a way that "God wants." These symbolic goals are often there but can be enhanced if we can help our clients articulate them.

Keeping These Goals Working. Whether it is getting rid of symptoms, recovering roles like being an employee or student, working for those we love, or proving something to ourselves or others, these positive reasons to recover often need to be enhanced if they are to fully motivate the person. Once I am clear on what positive reasons are motivating my client to recover, I try to follow a few key steps:

1. **Identify Them as a Key Goal, and Then Repeatedly Refer to Them.** I want my clients to think repeatedly about these positive motives and to remind themselves when I am not around. Our brains will naturally look for

risks—ways that we can lose things, and so it is extra important that we help keep a focus on the positive reasons for taking chances and working for recovery.

2. **If You Are Working with Clinicians, Help Them See These Positive Motives.** They may not understand what's motivating their client or may not be talking with them about their motives. You can help the clinical team all share what the person values most and what is driving their recovery.

3. **Tie Clinical Goals to These Personal Goals.** You want to make it clear how the goals of treatment are directly contributing to the person's overall positive hopes and goals. It is easier to try an unpleasant medication if we remember that we are trying to get rid of this depression so that we can return to a job we love or be a better parent. We can tolerate challenging psychotherapy if we are clear that it will get us closer to having better relationships with our family.

4. **Think About Your Work as a Peer as It Relates to Their Ultimate Goals.** Peers can talk about their experience with depression, but they can also offer valuable support when they talk about getting a career, graduating from college, getting married, or becoming a good parent. Clients need to know that these things are possible, and evidence from Peer Support Specialists who have achieved them will be convincing.

CHAPTER 8

THINKING ABOUT LEVELS OF CARE—WHERE TO HELP PEOPLE ENGAGE

Healthcare is complex and has many different places to engage. If we are not careful, people may engage at the wrong level of care, and thus not have a positive experience, and that may set back their efforts to seek help.

Picture healthcare as a large building with many doors. Behind each door is a different type of service, or "level of care." If we do not help people find the right door fairly early in their search, they are likely to stop looking. We need to know the levels of care and where to find them.

What are the most common levels of care for mental health conditions?

Inpatient Care - Psychiatric Hospitalization. This is the most intensive level of care and offers the highest level of control. Usually, people who are at imminent risk of hurting themselves or others, or who are experiencing acute psychotic/manic symptoms where they pose a safety risk to themselves or others, will be placed in a locked mental health inpatient unit. Because of the safety risk and the severity of the symptoms, the environment is very restrictive. People are not allowed to leave and activities may be very limited. The lack of freedom means that the situation is carefully governed by laws designed to minimize risk. These hospital stays are typically short, often lasting only three to five days. The focus of treatment is on keeping the person safe while they are stabilized. It is not designed to fully address the underlying clinical issues, and so the transition to other levels of care is critical. Most people never experience this level of care.

Residential Care. In this level of care, patients are living in the place where they are receiving treatment. Treatment is typically daily for many hours per day. Living at the program allows for relatively intense treatment while reducing the risk that the environment may pose. For some, residential care makes it less likely that they will use substances. For others, residential care makes it less likely that they will be involved with situations or people that contribute to their symptoms. This care is voluntary, and so the person is assumed to be able to make a good choice about whether care is beneficial for them. At the same time, program staff do provide twenty-four-hour monitoring and support.

Intensive Outpatient Programming (IOP). In general, receiving treatment in an IOP involves living at home while you attend treatment at least three (and often five) days a week, with at least three hours per day devoted to treatment. Participation often involves both group and individual treatment, and typically addresses a wide range of clinical and life issues. The intensity is designed for those clients who need treatment more than once or twice a week.

General Outpatient Care. This is the level of care most people think of when they think of mental health treatment. A client lives at home and may see a nurse practitioner or a psychiatrist for medication management. The patient may also go see a therapist or counselor once a week. The client is spending most of their time in their usual routine, and the treatment sessions are designed to help them address issues while they are living their lives.

Integrated Primary Care/Mental Healthcare. In recent years there has been rapid growth in the provision of mental healthcare within primary care. Often, mental health providers work alongside primary care doctors and nurses, providing short-term treatment for problems that are not considered severe enough to require ongoing outpatient mental healthcare. Examples of problems that are often treated in integrated primary care/mental healthcare include short-term crises, mild depression or anxiety, situational stressors, grief, and so on.

Self-Management, Self-Help, and Community-Based Peer Support. Many clinical problems are managed by people without ongoing professional help. Some people may know enough about how to manage their illness that they can do so on their own, or with the help of self-help books. Others may rely on

Figure 3: Levels of Care

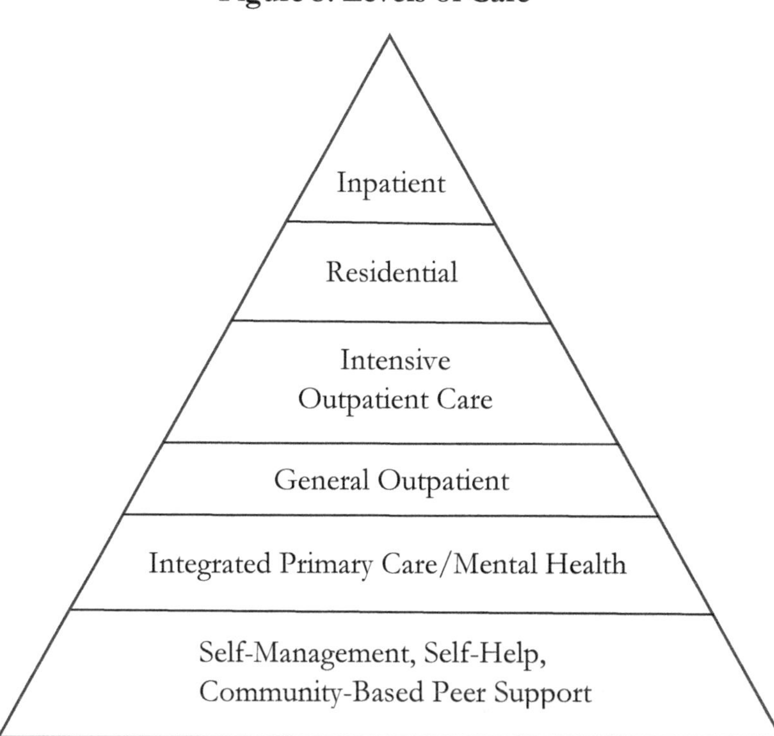

self-help or peer support groups where they work with others to manage their symptoms. This level of care is appropriate when the person has a good understanding of their illness and treatment, and can manage successful treatment without the regular input of a healthcare provider. Some people "graduate" to this level of care after they successfully participate in formal treatment. Others first try self-management, and then move on to formal care with a healthcare professional if self-management does not work.

PART II: TOOLS YOU CAN USE

CHAPTER 9

USE EXISTING PROGRAMMING DESIGNED TO HELP CLIENTS ENGAGE

There are existing efforts in place to encourage treatment and peer support engagement. If available, you will want to work with some of these. Some you may want to refer to. Others you should at least know about.

INFORMATION SHARING

This is the simplest form of assistance. Examples would include public service announcements on TV and radio, educational efforts designed to raise awareness of treatment and recovery in the community, tables at community events, written materials, and so on.

These strategies are helpful for people whose primary barrier to getting help is lack of knowledge. As we've talked about, most people have more barriers than simple lack of knowledge, and so information sharing alone is not effective with many people.

AUTOMATIC SCREENING AND REFERRAL

In these efforts, people are routinely screened for a clinical condition or a need for assistance, and if they are found to need help, they are routinely asked if they would like a referral. Often this is done by people that virtually everyone sees, such as by primary care doctors or by schools. This strategy has been shown to be very effective in getting people to the treatment they need and shortening the time to getting help. Such efforts work because they bypass the person's self-awareness, identifying the need and then encouraging the person to seek help.

Screening and referral tools are used for a wide range of health issues such as high blood pressure and cancer. For our purposes, we want to be aware of the fairly routine screenings done for substance use disorders, depression, suicidality, and PTSD.

These approaches always include:
1. Some kind of standard brief screening procedures— usually in the form of a few questions that have been found to identify a need for care.
2. When the screen is positive, there is usually some form of brief intervention, often consisting of a five- to twenty-minute conversation in which the screener provides information and advice regarding getting help. The key seems to be specific advice to get help and information about where and how to get it.

These strategies have been found to speed the process of help seeking. They do rely on the person's ability to recognize the problem when it is pointed out, and to take action when it is recommended. These strategies are less effective when someone is very ambivalent about getting help.

PRIMARY CARE WITH INTEGRATED MENTAL HEALTH

In the 1980s it was becoming clear that mental health conditions were often being treated by primary care doctors (Druss & Goldman, 2018). In the 1990s, the first study showed that integrating mental healthcare into primary care settings results in better care for many people, including earlier treatment for some conditions. This has now become a standard approach to primary care in many settings. You may have seen, as you talk with your primary care doctor, that they are listening for any sign you may need some form of mental healthcare. If they recognize a need, they then introduce you to "a colleague" in their clinic who can provide help. You don't have to go to a specific mental health clinic, and it may not even be mentioned that this colleague is a mental healthcare provider. If you do need specialized mental healthcare that the clinic does not have, then you are referred elsewhere.

This approach is very useful in many cases because it combines routine screening in a place that most people are seen routinely, with easy access to care, and little stigma. You are often just seeing a "colleague" down the hall from your primary care doctor. It is, of course, not effective for those who are not seen routinely in primary care. It is also ineffective for people who are well defended against getting help—they often continue to resist treatment regardless of who provides it.

INTENSIVE REFERRAL TO SELF-HELP GROUPS

Often simple referral by healthcare providers to needed services or peer support does not work. Researchers have been trying to find a more active referral process that results in greater success—with a particular focus on referral to peer support and self-help groups. The following broad strategies were found by researchers to result in significantly higher participation rates (Drebing et al., 2018). Each of these six steps has different options that you as a Peer Support Specialist or an outreach worker might choose, giving you some flexibility to develop strategies that work in different situations. You'll also note that Peer Support Specialists have a key role in this process, and so you may find yourself serving as the bridge.

As with all referrals, the intensive referral process should begin with a conversation between the referring clinician and their client. The clinician and/or Peer Support Specialist/outreach worker will explain the value of peer support and community connection and inquire about past experience in self-help/12-step meetings. If after the initial brief discussion, they think it is appropriate to make a referral, they choose at least one option under each of the following six strategies:

1. **Verbally Encourage Participation.**

- Recommend that the client attend at least a target number of meetings per week.

- Ask the client to set a personal goal to attend a target number of meetings.

- Mention the goal commonly stated in AA of "90 meetings in 90 days."

- Solicit and identify a specific goal for attendance (what group, when).

- Encourage the client to join a group or identify a possible sponsor.

2. **Provide Written Information.**
   - Provide the client with a list of meetings, with times, locations, and directions to those meetings (by foot, car, and public transportation).

   - Provide the client with a handout about self-help groups that includes summary information on their philosophy, structure, and terminology.

   - Provide the client with key reading material. An example would the "Big Book" for AA.

   - Provide the client with a list of local meetings preferred by other clients.

   - Provide the client with a list of common concerns of other clients about attending meetings.

   - Provide the client with a handout about obtaining a sponsor.

   - Provide the client with a list of currently available local sponsors.

3. **Arrange for a Group Member/Peer Support Specialist to Meet or Call the Client.**

- Ask the client for permission to invite a Peer Support Specialist who is familiar with that specific group to join the clinical session and pass along necessary information about connecting with self-help group members in their community. If they agree, have them sign a release of information and call the peer.

- Ask the client for permission to invite a Peer Support Specialist with experience with that group to contact them to introduce themselves and to arrange to meet them at a peer support meeting. If they agree, have them sign a release of information and call the peer.

- Ask the client for permission to invite a Peer Support Specialist from the group to contact them to introduce themselves and to provide a ride for the client to the meeting. If they agree, have them sign a release of information and call the peer.

4. **Ask for a Verbal or Written Commitment from the Client to Attend a Meeting.**
   - Ask the client to make a verbal or written commitment for meeting their attendance goals identified above

   - Ask the client to document attendance or reason for nonattendance in a journal.

   - Review the journal comments with the client during a subsequent meeting.

   - Ask the client to have the self-help group secretary document their attendance (ensure the client understands how to identify and approach the group secretary).

5. **Review and/or Practice Common Behaviors Needed During Attendance at Groups.**
    - In the clinical setting, create practice sessions/ simulations to expose the client to the group format and common behaviors by group members.

    - In the clinical setting, have the client participate in a practice group meeting or simulation.

    - Ask the client, "What might participation look like?" and ask if any discussion would be helpful.

6. **Follow Up After a Referral.**
    - After the client planned to attend a meeting, raise the topic of the client's experience. Discuss their impressions. If they did not attend, recommend attendance or ask for a recommitment to attend.

    - Raise the topic of the client's experience after several subsequent meetings.

    - Raise the topic of "getting active" in support groups (e.g., making comments in the meetings, getting support from others, asking for phone numbers, getting a sponsor). Encourage these steps.

ENGAGING FAMILY AND FRIENDS AS PARTNERS

Coaching Into Care. Families are often involved in decisions to enter mental healthcare. The VA has developed a specific program designed to enhance this role for family members and friends (Sayers, Hess, Whitted, Straits-Tröster & Glynn, 2021).

This approach seeks to provide family members with support and education so that they can be more effective at helping people make good decisions about seeking help. You may find that engaging a concerned family member will be key to your work with an ambivalent client. This tool can be valuable for helping guide those partners.

Coaching Into Care is a telephone-based service that works with concerned family members and friends of a veteran who is reluctant to enter needed care. It is set up like a call center, providing coaching to fifteen hundred to two thousand friends and family members per year.It is staffed by trained responders who are equipped to educate, counsel, and coach callers. Most callers are family members who are trying to motivate their relative to seek needed mental health support. Coaches typically provide education about mental illnesses, treatment, and strategies for navigating the healthcare system. They often use motivational interviewing strategies (see chapter 11) to help the friend or family member communicate.

Engaging family and friends can be uniquely helpful in your work, as they are the natural support networks for people who are well defended against getting help. This approach typically addresses the lack of insight by the person by engaging others to help build insight and to influence decision-making. It does depend on insightful family and/or friends, which some people do not have. You will want to use this strategy in situations where you see potential partners in families

CHAPTER 10

STRATEGIES FROM RESEARCH ON PERSUASION

The term *persuasion* can raise concerns in some clinical settings. We don't want to coerce people. We don't want to act like a used car salesperson pushing people to do something for our own benefit. If we take a step back, it is worth considering the formal definition. *Merriam-Webster* defines *persuasion* as the act or process of moving someone "by argument, entreaty, or discussion to a belief, position, or course of action." For our purposes, we are talking about acts that move people who need to seek help or participate in treatment or peer support through argument, entreaty, or expostulation. I would add that we are talking about moving people to do something that is in their own interest— something that will lead to or support their recovery. Coercion is not persuasion; coercion involves forcing people to do something. By fully respecting someone's responsibility to choose for themselves, we are using processes to help them make decisions that are in their interest. Those "processes" can vary widely, and that is what this chapter is about. The processes we are interested in are only those that are fully respectful of the person as the decider.

In 2017, Jay Conger wrote a valuable article in *Harvard Business Review* about common mistakes people make when they try to persuade others (Conger, 2017). These mistakes include:

1. **They Start With a "Hard Sell".** Conger points out that starting a conversation with elements of a 'hard sell' "gives potential opponents something to grab onto—and fight against."

2. **They Act as Though Persuasion Depends Only on Presenting Great Arguments.** Arguments and reasoning are only one part of the solution. "Other factors matter just as much, such as the persuader's credibility and his or her ability to create a proper, mutually beneficial frame for a position, connect on the right emotional level with an audience, and communicate through vivid language that makes arguments come alive."

3. **They Approach Persuasion as a One-Conversation Effort.** "More often than not, persuasion involves listening to people, testing a position, developing a new position that reflects input from the group, more testing, incorporating compromises, and then trying again."

4. **They Resist Any Compromise.** Too many people see compromise as surrender, but it is common and often essential. Before people change their view, they want to see that the other person is flexible enough to really consider and respond to their concerns. "By not compromising, ineffective persuaders unconsciously send

the message that they think persuasion is a one-way street."

We can build positive strategies based on these common mistakes about persuasion. Consider these eight principles of healthy, helpful persuasion:

Principle 1: Earn the Right to Speak by Listening. We often assume we have the right to give advice. That assumption is surprising because most people feel annoyed when other people give them unsolicited advice, but we often don't see that when we want to advise others. A key starting point is to recognize that we should have to earn the right to speak and share our views, and that we do so primarily by listening. Listening is the first message we give anyone. It communicates several key things:

- We respect them as the decider—this respect for their role has to be genuine.

- We have good intentions—we have their interest at heart.

- We understand them and their situation.

- We don't have ulterior motives.

Principle 2: Don't Assume—Ask and Learn. We start with listening because we need to understand the other person and the situation. Asking and being curious is similar to listening. It provides us the information we need to truly understand the situation. It also communicates our respect for them and for the issue we are discussing. Making assumptions simply communicates disrespect and undercuts our credibility.

Principle 3: Help the Other Person Connect with What Is Most Important for Them and How Treatment Would Support That. Helping people talk about what is most important to them sets the stage for an open discussion about whether getting help supports those values. It is not uncommon for us to have a disconnect between the decisions we make each day and our ultimate values and goals. By asking about ultimate values and goals, we allow the person to say out loud what they want in their lives. Getting help is often a key step toward achieving those goals or living out those values. If you frame your inquiry correctly, they will often say that they want X, and they know they need help to address their barriers.

Principle 4: Stay Calm, Patient, and Supportive of the Person. We have all seen people get frustrated with us when we don't do what they want. We don't want to be that person; it often closes down the opportunity to persuade. If we are truly supportive of the person as the decision-maker, we know that persuasion is almost never a single discussion. Help seeking is a very complex process, and making the decision to reach out takes time and processing. Getting frustrated or impatient is often seen as disrespectful and ends the discussion.

Principle 5: Ask for Permission to Share Information. After you've proved that you understand their view and situation and that you don't have other agendas, ask if you can share information. The simple process of asking permission goes a long way to communicate respect for them and recognition that you are only offering something for them to consider. It may feel odd to ask at first, but you'll want to get in the habit of doing this routinely. I have never had anyone say "no". Once someone agrees to your providing information, it is easier for them to really listen to it. There is also evidence that when people say yes to a small request ("Is it OK if I share some information about that treatment?"), they are more likely to say yes to larger requests, which can be valuable as your conversation continues.

Principle 6: Let Them See Success in You and Others. Too often we have to make decisions about healthcare without enough formal information, particularly about the success rates of available treatments. Those who have been in treatment may have seen many others in treatment failing to change. They don't see the successful cases—typically because people who have successfully participated in treatment are not in treatment anymore, and so are not as available. This creates a natural illusion that treatment doesn't work ("Everyone in this program has relapsed before—I don't think anyone really recovers"). You need to fight this belief by making success more visible to those you are working with. Consider the following strategies:

- Introduce them to other individuals who have succeeded.

- Introduce them to groups of people succeeding—support groups.

- Develop and share stories of success, yours and others.

- Get comfortable talking about your own successes, not for the attention or praise, but to provide evidence to the people you are working with.

Principle 7: Reduce the Unknowns. People don't like the unknown and will overestimate bad things when there are unknowns. We often are not aware of what our clients **don't** know—and so **we don't address** it. You can help fill in the unknown areas by using a few simple guidelines:

- Know and talk about what happens when they first enter treatment.

- Know and talk about what is involved in participating in treatment over time.

- Know and talk about what the success rates are.

- Know and talk about what success looks like (what symptoms remain, what functioning returns, what life is like in recovery).

Principle 8: Refer to Authorities They Value. Different people are persuaded by different types of authorities. Some want to hear about research while others want to know about what celebrities recommend. We can differ in what we see as the best authorities, but if our goal is to help people move toward recovery, it will be practical if we can talk about the full range of authorities so that we are mostly likely to provide information they will respect. These sources include:

- Other people like them.

- Well-known people with the same issue.

- Researchers.

- Authorities such as doctors, nurses, religious leaders, and others.

- Published books and articles.

Your work in helping others engage in needed treatment is essentially a task of persuasion. You already have some skills in persuasion, but over time you will become an expert in persuading others to take steps that support their recovery. These eight principles of effective persuasion will take years to fully implement and understand, but they will become the core of your work.

CHAPTER 11

STRATEGIES FROM MOTIVATIONAL INTERVIEWING

Motivational interviewing (MI) refers to a counseling approach that was developed for working with people struggling with substance use disorders. It is designed to encourage behavior change by helping clients explore and resolve ambivalence about making a change (Miller & Rollnick, 2012). We talked a little about MI in chapter 5, but now we will look at it in more detail.

MI is now being used with a wide range of clinical and nonclinical behaviors: some people will use it as part of psychotherapy, while others use it to help people make decisions about non-clinical issues such as their insurance. You would be using it as an outreach tool and not as a clinical intervention. The approach includes a number of useful concepts that are very relevant to help seeking, and particularly to the effort to persuade others to seek needed supports. You will see overlap with the content in other chapters, but the overall model has a unique perspective that is now widely used in clinical and nonclinical settings.

1. **Approach the Person with a Stance of Respect.** A basic assumption of MI is that the person you are trying to persuade is, and should be, responsible for making their own decisions. A common mistake is to try to override or undercut that person's responsibility for those decisions in order to push them toward what we see as the "right" decision. Anything that undercuts their responsibility communicates disrespect and usually results in no change and broken rapport.

2. **Anticipate Ambivalence About Change.** MI starts with the assumption that all people are ambivalent about most decisions, even if they don't or can't explicitly express their ambivalence. In trying to help others make good decisions, it is usually safe to assume that ambivalence is present and that it is helpful to talk openly about it. If they have trouble talking about their ambivalence, they may need your help thinking openly and nonjudgmentally about their thoughts and feelings related their decision.

3. **Make Ambivalence Explicit.** To help others make any change, it is often useful to assist them in making their ambivalence fully explicit so they can see it. This includes helping them openly state their specific feelings and thoughts for and against *making the change* and *not making the change*. As we talked about in chapter 5, MI uses a tool called a motivational matrix, developed to help clients identify and organize the costs and benefits of changing and not changing. This tool is very helpful for clarifying ambivalence and improving decisions.

Figure 4 provides the basic format for a motivational matrix as well as two completed examples: one for talking to a provider about entering mental health treatment and one for entering a community-based peer support group. In some settings, outreach workers may simply want to use the logic of the motivational matrix in conversation instead of actually filling out the table on paper. In other settings it may be helpful to actually create a written document that the person can take with them. Regardless of the format, your goal is to help the person openly consider all the costs and benefits of changing versus not changing.

Figure 4: Examples of Motivational Matrixes

Example 1: Blank Motivational Matrix

	Making the Change	No Change
Costs and Lost Opportunities		
Benefits		

Example 2: Completed Motivational Matrix

Target Change: Talk to My Primary Care Doctor About My Depression

	Making the Change	**No Change**
Costs and Lost Opportunities	1. Embarrassment of bringing this up. 2. Might have to start therapy, which will take time and could interfere with my work.	1. I will continue to feel depressed. 2. I will continue to feel like I'm not being a good wife & mother. 3. I will continue to be distant from my friends. 4. I will continue to feel bad about myself. 5. I will continue to have terrible sleep. 6. Health risks from depression
Benefits	1. I could stop feeling so hopeless and sad. 2. I could be the involved parent and wife I used to be. 3. I would have more fun and more friends again. 4. I would do better at work—maybe make more money.	1. I could avoid thinking about the overwhelming problems in my past. 2. I could keep focused on what I'm doing right now.

Example 3: Completed Motivational Matrix
Target Change: To Start Attending a Parents Anonymous Group

	Making the Change	**No Change**
Costs and Lost Opportunities	1. Having to meet new people. I feel anxious in social settings. 2. The embarrassment of talking about the problems at home. 3. My schedule is very busy. Can I afford the time?	1. I will continue to see my kids having problems, which could be permanent. 2. I feel I can't talk about these problems with anyone, and I'll continue to feel this way. 3. I'll continue to feel like a bad parent; it makes me depressed.
Benefits	1. I could get new ideas about how to deal with these parenting issues. 2. I would not feel so alone. 3. I could make some new friends. 4. I could get a little time away from home; it could help with my stress.	1. I can keep up my current schedule of activities. 2. I won't feel embarrassed about these problems if I don't have to talk about them.

4. Help Them Consider the Full Range of the Benefits of Change and the Costs of Failing to Change. All four sections, or "quadrants," of the motivational matrix are important, but researchers have found that two quadrants are the most important for encouraging change: (1) the benefits of making the change and (2) the costs and lost opportunities of not making the change. You'll want to help your clients think about the items in each quadrant but particularly the items in those two. Consider the following categories of benefits for making a change:

- How will reducing or eliminating symptoms feel?

- What areas of functioning will improve (e.g., work, school, parenting, friends, intimate relationships)?

- How will others see them?

- What would feel like the "right" thing to do?

- What are indirect benefits that may result from seeking help?

- How does the change help the person get things they really want in life?

- How does the change help the person avoid or resolve negative things?

5. **Create Conversations That Encourage the Other Person to Talk About Changing.** One of the best predictors of whether people will make a change is the amount of time they spend talking about how the change would help them and how not making the change would be negative. It is not how much *we* talk about it, but how much *they* talk about it. If we talk in such a way that the other person is encouraged to talk about making the change, that change is more likely to happen. Sometimes I have pushed too aggressively for a change, and the other person naturally tends to feel defensive, and then talks about the reasons they don't want to make the change. In those situations, I've

made it less likely that the person will change. Look for ways to encourage the other person to talk about making the change.

6. **"Roll with Resistance."** This phrase was coined by the founders of MI to describe a very common point in these conversations: when the person talks about wanting to not change or gives reasons not to change. I often feel tempted to then push harder for change, which is exactly the wrong step. By "rolling with resistance," we should not counter resistance by increasing the arguments for making the change. Instead, we should use those statements of resistance to help the other person further explore the problem. "Rolling with resistance" avoids causing the other person to dig in to that stance of resisting change and keeps the conversation going.

7. **Talk About the Importance of the Change.** Our clients may agree that a change should happen, but that does not mean that they will take action. Most people face many competing concerns in their lives, and the need for change may not be the most pressing issue for them. Once they have agreed that they want to take a step to get help, we need to ask about how important the change is to them. To what degree is it a priority, relative to the other competing issues? For example, MI suggests we ask, "From 1 to 10, where is this change on your priority list?" If the priority is fairly low, the advocate's job now shifts to increasing the perceived importance of this change, using the persuasion skills described in other chapters.

8. **Talk About How Confident They Feel About Making the Change.** You will want to routinely ask how confident they are that they can successfully make the change. They may not feel they know how to start a treatment or find a good peer support group. They may have failed in the past. Most people avoid trying things they feel are likely to result in failure and so will not try to make a change if they don't believe they have the skill or

resources to do it. For example, the advocate may say, "How confident do you feel that you can find a therapist and make a first appointment?" If confidence is not high, the conversation shifts to identifying the perceived barriers to feeling confident and determining how those barriers can be addressed.

9. **Recognize the Signs of Success.** You will want to become very good at recognizing the signs that efforts to persuade someone to seek help are succeeding. These signs typically include the person doing one of three things: (1) talking about the desire to seek help, (2) expressing that getting help is highly important to them, or (c) expressing feeling confident that they can reach out and get help.

CHAPTER 12

STRATEGIES FROM COGNITIVE BEHAVIORAL THERAPY

The term *cognitive behavioral therapy* (CBT) typically refers to one of the most common forms of psychotherapy, used for a wide range of mental health and behavioral conditions (Butler, Chapman, Forman & Beck, 2006). CBT also represents a useful framework or theory for thinking about people and behavior. It is now as widely as a framework as it is a form of psychotherapy, and is commonly available to laypeople via books and web-based material.

CBT represents a fairly simple but practical model of human behavior. It emphasizes the value of thinking about people in three general dimensions: behaviors, thoughts, and feelings. These three dimensions interact with each other, each being influenced by and influencing the others. Because thoughts may be the most modifiable, efforts to change often focus first on them. CBT holds that thoughts are often tied to core beliefs about yourself, others, and the future. To change our thoughts, we need to understand and work with those core beliefs.

CBT AND HELP SEEKING

Treatment engagement is a behavior like any other, and so CBT says it is tied to our thoughts and feelings. Common feelings related to help seeking include hope about feeling better, anxiety about asking for help, shame of needing help, and fear of what treatment could lead to. Common thoughts tied to core beliefs include ideas we have about whether it is "right" or "good" to seek help versus solving problems "by myself" and beliefs about the likelihood that asking others for help will lead to a positive outcome (Yurica & DiTomasso, 2005). Both feelings and thoughts can represent barriers to getting the help we (or others) need. Again, we will focus on thoughts as they tend to be easier to change.

COMMON COGNITIVE DISTORTIONS

We want to watch for ways that our clients are thinking about help seeking that are based on flawed logic. These include:

1. **All-or-Nothing Thinking.** This distortion is also referred to as *black-and-white thinking* and reflects a common tendency to see things as simply all good or all bad, or all right or all wrong. Reality is rarely so simple, and so this distortion reflects a tendency to not see shades of gray that exist in most elements of real life. With treatment engagement, your client may see **themselves as either "strong" or "weak."** Any recognition of symptoms of depression or anxiety would make the person see themselves as "weak." Any involvement in any mental healthcare would make them see themselves like a "failure."

Examples of Things You Can Say to Challenge All-or-Nothing Thinking:
"You seem to see yourself as either all good or all bad. Could it be that there is something in the middle?"

"Could it be that you may have some feelings of depression or anxiety and not be a totally weak person?"

"Abraham Lincoln and Winston Churchill both talked about feeling very depressed at times. Do you think they were weak people?"

2. **Overgeneralization.** In this distortion, people take one instance or example and inappropriately generalize it to an overall pattern. With treatment or peer support, the person may take an example of one experience with an uncaring provider and generalize that all healthcare providers are uncaring. They may take one negative experience at a peer support group and conclude that all peer support groups are terrible.

Things You Can Say to Challenge Overgeneralizations:
"So, because Dr. Johnson turned out to be a jerk, do you think every doctor is a jerk? That doesn't fit with my experience."

"You may be right that there are some uncaring doctors, but my experience is that most are pretty good and many are wonderful. The uncaring doctors are relatively rare."

"Sounds like that peer support group had a lot of conflict. Many are not like that. I am aware of many others. Would you be willing to try some other groups?"

3. **Mental Filter.** In this distortion, people focus on negative data and exclude all positive data. For example, your client decides to go to a 12-step meeting for the first time. They had previously been told by a friend that these meetings are "just people telling war stories." The meeting includes ten different people talking, many of them sharing genuine current struggles. One of the speakers does share old war stories. Your client leaves the meeting saying, "My friend was right. It is all just people telling war stories. I'm never going back to that meeting!"

Things You Can Say to Challenge Mental Filters: "How many people talked at the meeting? How many told war stories? I've heard of some of that at times, but most meetings I've gone to had a lot of good comments as well."

"Let's talk to Justin and Tara. They go to a lot of meetings. They can tell us about their experience about meetings and war stories."

"You seem to be looking for negative things to focus on to give you a reason not to go. Could that be true?"

4. **Control Fallacy.** People engage in the control fallacy by thinking either (a) "I'm in total control" or (b) "I have no control." Neither is typically true, and both are destructive. For help seeking, people may feel that they don't need to seek help because they have no control over important things in their life. Similarly, they may feel they don't need help because they are entirely in control, and so won't benefit from help.

Things You Can Say to Challenge the Control Fallacy:

"Sounds like you feel you have no control over anything in your life. Is that right? That must be a scary way to feel. How can you solve any problem if you have no control?"

"You may not have control of some things, but you do have control of others. Can we talk about what you can do?"

"Sounds like you don't think anything will help you. I wonder why so many other people find these groups helpful."

"If you have so much control over your life, why are things going the way they are? Maybe others could help you improve your control?"

5. **Personalization.** In this fallacy, the individual takes everything personally. In one very common version, the person feels they are to blame for everything, even when there is no logical link between their action and the outcome. For help seeking, a person may feel that they are to blame for the problems that are precipitating their anxiety or depression, and so their suffering is deserved ("Why get help when I deserve this?"). Someone who is entering treatment may misinterpret small hiccups that occur as something personal. For example, the therapist calls to reschedule the first session, and the client thinks this is about them: "They don't want to work with me." "They don't like me."

Things You Can Say to Challenge Personalization:
"So your doctor rescheduled your appointment? What do you think that means? Could it be she was just busy and

had to shift her schedule? That is pretty common in my experience."

"Sounds like you feel your mental health condition is your own fault—that you are to blame. Could it be that the illness is making you feel guilty? Most of these illnesses are related to biological problems. How can you be to blame for a biological problem?"

"You seem to think everything is about you. That is surprising. I find that most of the time people's actions toward me are really about them."

6. ***Should* Statements.** It is common for people to make statements to themselves about what they "should" do or be able to do. These statements often reflect unrealistic expectations, such as "I should be able to cope with this stress without help," and "My doctor should be able to know what I need without my having to say it."

Things You Can Say to Challenge Overreliance on *Should* Statements:
"You use the word *should* a lot. I certainly can't do all the things you expect of yourself, and the people I know couldn't live up to those expectations either. Sounds unrealistic to me."

"Do you think that it is realistic that your doctor should be able to tell what is going on without your telling them?"

7. **Emotional Reasoning.** This is a common but illogical way that people can draw conclusions ("I feel it; therefore, it must be true"). We often feel things that are not true. If we act on those feelings, we can create all

kinds of problems. In healthcare decisions, people can draw emotional conclusions about care based on their feelings instead of the reality of the care, such as "If I talk to a mental health clinician, then I'm afraid I'll go crazy," or "If I say that I'm feeling suicidal to another person, then I will be more likely to lose control and kill myself."

Things You Can Say to Challenge Emotional Reasoning:
"You are afraid if you go to talk with a psychologist, you'll go crazy. You may feel that way, but I don't think it works that way. I've never seen that in all the people I've ever worked with. Could it be you've gotten that wrong, and going to see someone will actually be the first step to solving your challenges?"

"You are afraid to say you want to hurt yourself because you may then hurt yourself? I'm pretty sure that researchers have found that is simply not true. You may be afraid that you'll lose control, but the researchers say that talking about it is not likely to cause loss of control, but more often helps."

"I'm not sure you're thinking very clearly about this. How about we run this by a few other peers to see how they think about it?"

8. **Fortune Telling.** This distortion is related to emotional reasoning. "I feel discouraged about my present and so I conclude that my future will be the same." "I haven't been able to stay sober for more than a day, and so I'll never be able to be sober." "I have tried medication for depression and it hasn't worked, so I will never find one that will help me." We are often trying to protect

ourselves from disappointment, but actually we are undercutting our hope and our options.

Things You Can Say to Challenge Fortune Telling: "How do you know what is going to happen? Can you tell the future? Lots of people have to try many treatments before they find one that works. They didn't know what would work, but they persevered until they got the recovery they wanted."

"Your view of your future is not very realistic. Would you be willing to talk to a few of my colleagues about how they thought about their future before they started recovery and how they think about it now?"

9. **Mind Reading.** This is similar to fortune telling. We draw conclusions about what others think or feel based on our impressions or our guesses instead of actual information. The problem is that even when we know others well, we are often wrong when we make assumptions about what they think. "I tried to go to AA. I could tell that everyone at the meeting thought I didn't fit in and wished I wasn't there." "My husband thinks I shouldn't see the doctor because I'm just feeling sorry for myself. He hasn't said that but I can tell he thinks it."

Things You Can Say to Challenge Mind Reading: "Sounds like you are doing a little mind reading there. How do you know what they were thinking—did you ask? I have found that my own guesses at what others are feeling are often completely wrong. That's why I almost always ask people and I don't trust my guesses."

"You think your husband feels you shouldn't see the doctor. Have you asked him that? Did he say that? You might be wasting a lot of time and energy by guessing. Just ask him honestly."

10. **Disqualifying the Positive.** In this particularly painful distortion, the person takes a positive experience and then rejects the experience by explaining it away. "The doctor said he sees improvement in my depression, but I know he doesn't mean it—he is saying that just to encourage me." "Someone at the NAMI group gave a compliment on my comments; that is just because they want something from me."

Things You Can Say to Challenge Disqualifying the Positive:

"Do you see what you did there? You just undercut the feedback your doctor gave you. Could it be that he was telling you the truth—that you are improving? Do you often have trouble accepting success?"

"Could it be that they were sincere in complimenting you? Is that fair to yourself to explain away compliments from others?"

CORE BELIEFS

Core beliefs represent a key element in the CBT perspective (Wenzel, 2012). These are ideas or philosophies that we all hold very strongly and very deeply. We may not even be aware that we hold them, but they impact how we respond to situations, such as when we have symptoms or problems that we could use help with. These beliefs are usually developed early in our lives and can be negative or positive.

Core beliefs that are formed during childhood can be reinforced by later experiences. For example, I may have developed a core belief that I have to solve all my problems by myself. I learned this because I grew up on a farm, and my parents always said, "You have to take care of everything yourself. No one is going to help you in life." I never saw them ask for help or talk about any mental health symptoms.

Core beliefs are typically global and absolute. I may continue to act, think, and feel as though that core belief is true, even if that was not what my parents meant. Core beliefs give rise to rules (never talk about your problems to others) or assumptions (people don't want to hear about my problems). These are reflected in automatic thoughts that we don't even recognize we have.

Core beliefs fall into three general but related categories: beliefs about yourself, other people, and the world. Watch out for some of these problematic beliefs:

Beliefs About Yourself
- I am entirely self-sufficient. I don't need help from anyone else.

- I don't deserve good things, including good health or support from others.

- I am special; I am entitled to things that others are not. I'm better than others; if people criticize me, they are bad.

- I have to take care of myself alone; no one else can or will.

- If I need anything from others, I'm bad, lazy, selfish, unlovable, incompetent, and so on.

- I am doomed to lead a life of sickness.

- Any show of weakness will result in terrible things.

- If I get to trust other people, including healthcare providers, they will let me down or leave me.

- Everything that happens is my fault.

- I am fragile. If anything changes or I try to change anything, my life/health will fall apart.

Beliefs About Other People

- People are going to let me down or hurt me.

- People don't want to be helpful.

- People are not competent; they can't help me.

- People will only help me in order to get something from me.

- People will never actually care about me.

Beliefs About the World

- In life, people get what they deserve; if people are sick, then they deserve it.

- The world doesn't have good things for me.

- Things must always be fair for everyone.

- The world, including every situation, is a dangerous place.

Common Strategies for Responding to Unhealthy Core Beliefs:

- Look for and point out core beliefs. Often, saying them out loud will help the person realize how unrealistic they are.

- When appropriate, point out the illogical nature of the belief. It is important to do this in a tactful and supportive way.

- When appropriate, ask about other people: "Do you think other people think that?" "Do you think I think that way?" Use your own views, and those of other peers, to help correct their beliefs.

- If appropriate, point out the logical implications of their belief: "So you **need to be totally self-sufficient**—you **can't ask for help.** So how does that fit with the rest of your life? Do you fix your own car? Do you fix your own broken arm?"

- In general, ask clarifying questions that spotlight their illogical conclusions. Again, this has to be done tactfully, and often repeated over time.

- Offer data that is inconsistent with their conclusions. Draw out the distinction between what they believe and what the reality is.

- Tell a recovery story that spotlights the same errors in thinking. Recovery stories about distorted thinking can be key to helping others recognize their own filters.

A Specific Intervention You May Want to Learn

CBT for Treatment Seeking (CBT-TS) is a brief (30–60 minute), single-session intervention that has been developed for use by Peer Support Specialists, outreach workers, and others (Possemato, Johnson, Wray, Webster & Stecker, 2018; Stecker, McHugo, Xie, Whyman & Jones, 2014). It is designed to help people make good decisions about seeking help and uses the principles we've talked about to support them. It contains three core elements: (1) identifying beliefs about seeking professional help, (2) generating alternative beliefs about seeking professional help, and (3) creating a plan for treatment.

This intervention involves a single conversation with someone who is ambivalent about entering a needed clinical service. Researchers have found that CBT-TS is associated with up to 50 percent of participants entering needed care. If you are interested, I would suggest you read the articles referenced above about this unique intervention.

CHAPTER 13

STRATEGIES FROM NARRATIVE THERAPY

Narrative therapy is an approach to psychotherapy more than a specific therapy. It has been described by a range of practitioners (Freedman & Combs, 1996; Madigan, 2011; White & Epston, 1990), all of whom have talked about the value of stories in understanding clients and recovery. Their perspective is very valuable to explaining people's behavior when it comes to seeking help, participating in treatment, and getting involved in peer support. Like CBT, narrative therapy is now used more broadly than just to guide therapy—and is available to you as a Peer Support Specialist to understand your clients and how best to provide effective peer support.

Basic Assumptions of Narrative Therapy:
1. People are naturally oriented toward stories and narrative. We automatically create stories out of our experience. Sometimes those stories are helpful, but they can also

result in problems. For example, we may notice we are having more disagreements with our work supervisor. We are likely to start creating a story to explain this change. This often happens before we even recognize it. If the story includes accurate information about the cause of the conflicts (e.g. "my boss is under stress right now"), it can guide good decisions on our part. If the story reflects inaccurate information (e.g. "my boss is trying to push me out"), we can make bad decisions with negative consequences.

2. Our stories reflect the stories told by the groups we belong to, including family, work groups, communities, countries, religions, and cultures. The scientific community, the self-help community, and the clinical community all use stories heavily in how they understand mental health problems, solutions to those problems, and the process of recovery.

3. Stories are not "objective truth" but constructed ideas that can have value in explaining things or giving direction to actions. Multiple stories explaining the same experiences can, and often do, exist simultaneously and can be useful in different ways. The concept that only one story can be "true" is a story in itself and is often not helpful.

4. Problems occur when the stories people have about themselves do not fit with their lived experience. The mismatch between the stories and the experience can cause confusion and stress. It is often a sign that the stories need to change to include new or different experiences.

5. The concepts of mental illnesses, often portrayed as real scientific entities, are seen as part of a story.   They are typically only one of the stories available to people that explain their difficulties. The concepts of illness, treatment, and recovery are often integrated in the stories that healthcare providers tell.   It is important to understand how people view these concepts if we want to understand the stories they hold about getting help and recovery.

6. Some people can get into difficult places when their lives have become tied too closely to a single story that is either limiting and/or superficial rather than multiple stories or more complex and nuanced stories.

7. Recovery always involves people changing the story/stories that they are using to understand themselves and their lives.

8. Effective clinical treatment and peer support involve ways of helping people change their stories so that recovery is supported. Participation in treatment and peer support can have direct benefits, but also creates benefits by being part of a story of change.

Recovery often involves the person engaging in what are called "individualized conversations," whereby they are invited by clinicians, peers, and others to consider their problems not as signs of an individualized deficit or pathology—something that was their fault—but rather as lying outside themselves. The clinician, peer, and client are thus united in a story focusing on a struggle against a problem that is "external." The person is not the problem, changing the common sense of failure people start the recovery process with.

Narrative therapy represents a move away from a simple story of a linear cause-and-effect model of care, where the role of the expert is to find out and fix the problem. People using narrative therapy prefer stories framed in terms of various internal and external "factors" that have resulted in the experience of "problems."

NARRATIVE AND PEER SUPPORT SPECIALISTS

From a narrative perspective, Peer Support Specialists have a very important role:

1. Peers have shared experience with clients, and so their perspective and stories are seen as particularly valuable, credible, and useful to clients. They often have more leverage than clinicians in helping clients change their narratives.

2. Peers also typically have more personal experience than clinicians with recovery and treatment. They have encountered some of the likely challenges that clients will face, and so hold key information clients need. This added experience exerts a strong influence on the stories of clients who have less, and maybe no, prior experience with recovery and treatment. Peers are often seen as the "experts" on the experience of recovery and treatment participation, and their recovery stories can serve as direct models of new stories for clients.

3. Clients who work only with professionals and have little or no contact with other people in recovery often have stories that reflect that lack of exposure to the way people actually recover. Likewise, many professionals have limited exposure to people in long-term recovery, working mostly with people in the early stages. They have

limited ability to help people develop that larger perspective on recovery.

4. Conversations between Peer Support Specialists and clients can be seen as efforts to compare, reanalyze, and rewrite the stories of both the client and the peer.

5. Peers often introduce clients to other peers and other groups of people in recovery. All these people can help expand the stories that clients tell, creating a larger focus on the recovery element of the story.

STRATEGIES FOR USING NARRATIVES TO ENCOURAGE ENTRY INTO TREATMENT AND PEER SUPPORT

1. Give People a Chance to Tell Their Story from Their Perspective. Start with their current version of their story. Listen to the events and people they include—and leave out. Listen for how the story points to the role they play. Are they causing all the problems? Are they impacting the problems? Are they helpless in the face of the problems? Listen to the values emphasized in the story.

2. Share Your Story About Your "Illness" and Recovery from Your Perspective. Be thoughtful about your own story, including what events and people you include, what role you played, and what values you emphasize. Your recovery stories will be key to how you help your clients, and so you want to be very thoughtful in how you construct them. Consider getting detailed feedback from your peers and supervisors about your recovery stories.

3. Help Introduce Clients to Others in Recovery Who Are Willing to Share Their Own Stories. Each additional story

will enhance the client's story. The more real stories of recovery they hear, the more hope they will have about their own recovery. They will also take lessons from each story, including the differences between the stories.

4. Help the Client See That the Problem Is, to a Large Extent, Outside of Themselves. This perspective can help them recognize that the problem is not them as a person but something they can choose to address and solve. Seeing mental illness as parallel to other physical illnesses can help with this. I often make parallels to illnesses like arthritis or chronic heart disease, chronic illnesses that can have a relapsing pattern like many mental illnesses. There are links to behavior, but most people don't see any stigma or personal shame in having arthritis or heat disease. As a model of illness, it can break the underlying story that mental illness is really about the failure of the person. It does not mean that the person is not responsible; indeed, this framework requires that the person take responsibility for having the illness and making good decisions to manage it. This is the next part of the story.

5. Help the Client See Things They Are Leaving Out of the Story, Including What Choices They Made and the Thinking Behind Their Actions. As you hear clients tell their stories, you'll naturally recognize gaps in what they include. At the right time, it is fairly easy to express curiosity or surprise that they didn't include some factor that may be important. By encouraging them to consider how they are constructing their story, you'll help them change it.

6. Help the Client See Their Own Strengths, Particularly as They Relate to What They Have Done or What They

Could Do. Clients often leave out their strengths, talents, and the good choices they have made. Pointing these out can help them add more balance to their story.

7. Point Out the Factors That Are Outside the Person's Control, Particularly Those Elements They May Seem to be Taking Responsibility For. The logic behind the Serenity Prayer is such a valuable reference point to guide us and our clients about this critical challenge in living: "God, grant me the serenity to accept the things I cannot change, the courage to change the things I can, and the wisdom to know the difference." We all struggle to live in a way that is consistent with this distinction between what we can change and what we have no control over. Clients will often show their struggles in how they tell their story, giving you an opportunity to point those struggles out.

8. Point Out Factors That Are Within the Person's Control. Emphasize their ability to decide and choose. Be curious about times they did not choose and why they didn't. Weave this into their story, as they will need to take action if their recovery is to be real.

9. Point Out Other Interpretations Than Those in the Story They Tell. I find I am often tempted to do this too quickly. I try to wait until the client has fully told me their story and they appear to feel that I really understand. When they know that, they will be more open to any comment from me offering a different interpretation of their experience. In this step you are basically suggesting they change their story. It can be a big step for them, and so do this cautiously.

10. Emphasize Shared Experience the Client Has with Others. Many illnesses make people feel alone, and people's stories can emphasize that sense of being alone or misunderstood. The reality is that many people are going through the same thing, and feeling alone is an unfortunate misunderstanding of their experience. They are not alone. It can also be helpful to point out the support that they could potentially have from family, friends, and others struggling with the same issues.

11. When Appropriate, Point Out How the Mental Illness May Be Coloring the Story. For example, a person struggling with depression may tell a story that is particularly hopeless or in which they portray themselves as incapable of taking any steps to get help. Peer Support Specialists can help the client see that the depression is creating that part of the story, and that there is more hope and competence than their depression is allowing them to see.

12. Use Metaphors to Reframe Their Stories to Point to Recovery and Hope. Metaphor can be a powerful tool to help people quickly change their stories. For example, I've often told clients who are just learning to take responsibility for their decisions: "Your life is a book with many chapters and pages. Every day is a new page. You write your own story." There are many helpful metaphors, and you'll want to pick those you find useful for your clients. I have found web-based lists helpful (https://mindremakeproject.org/2020/09/25/powerful-therapy-metaphors/). Over time, you'll accumulate a collection that works for you.

COMMON NARRATIVES THAT DISCOURAGE HELP SEEKING

There are common patterns in people's life narratives that lead them to avoid getting needed help. These include:

- I am a strong, virtuous person. Strong, virtuous people do not seek help from others, because seeking help is a sign of being weak or non-virtuous.

- If I seek help, I am betraying my faith, my family, my approach to life.

- Seeking help means that the problem is more serious than I think it is.

- If I seek help, I will fall apart. My problems will get more control over me, and I will no longer be able to function.

- If I seek help, I will lose control over my life. Whoever I see will take control of my decisions, and I will turn into someone else.

- If I seek help, I will lose control. I have to tell the other person everything and share everything. They will shame me or judge me.

- If I seek help, I will lose control. The person I seek help from will dictate what I must do, and if they are not good, I will be stuck with them.

You will want to listen for and challenge these patterns. They can be in the background when clients tell their stories, so you may have to listen particularly hard to hear them. Help the client become aware of these assumptions by asking questions, and point out the inaccuracy under these storylines.

CHAPTER 14

STRATEGIES FROM MORAL REASONING THEORY

Theories are tools more than complete representations of reality. I've noticed that some theories are very useful for some tasks, and so I use them, just like the hammer and wrench that I am always using out of my actual toolbox.

Lawrence Kohlberg's theory of moral reasoning (Kohlberg & Hersh, 1977) is a theory that I find very useful. It has been around for more than fifty years and was developed to describe different stages that people pass through as they grow in their moral decision-making from a small child to an adult. Subsequent research has found that this theory is overly simplistic and that people develop in a more varied pattern.

Despite this, I still use the stages because they are useful in creating a set of arguments that tend to move people toward a decision that is good for them. First, let's go over the stages:

Stage 1: Focus on Obedience and Avoidance of Punishment. The person focuses on what punishment might occur and makes decisions on how to act based on the desire to avoid punishment.

Stage 2: Focus on Self-Interest—What Do I Want? The person decides how to act by focusing on what they want and can get. What is right or wrong is determined by what they want.

Stage 3: Focus on What the Majority of People Think Is Right—Conformity with Expectations. The person sees what is right and wrong as determined by what the majority of other people think. Here, how to act is guided by peer pressure, public opinion, and what others are doing.

Stage 4: Focus on Authority and Social Order—What Do the Authorities and Social Order Require? The person makes decisions on how to act based on what the overall rules and authorities say should be done. There is a focus on guidelines, and recommendations from those in leadership roles.

Stage 5: Focus on the "Social Contract"—Balance of Rules and Individual Rights in the Service of the Larger Group. The person sees that what the community needs is important but is also balanced by what the individual needs. What is right is what benefits the most people.

Stage 6: Focus on Universal Ethical Principles Such as Love and Truth. The person uses abstract reasoning and values to determine their actions. Think about Gandhi or Martin Luther King and the way their higher ethical values argued for change, even when it conflicted with what the authorities or the larger peer groups thought was right.

Practically, I find this theory useful for constructing requests to those who have the authority to decide about resources and policies. It is also relevant in helping our clients think about the "right" thing to do for their recovery when it comes to engaging in peer support or in formal treatment. Given that people can operate in different stages at the same time, I would suggest that we develop our rationales to reflect all six stages. For example:

Assume you are working with a client who is struggling with a long history of depression and alcohol abuse. This has had a very negative impact on their life: They have lost several jobs because of it. Most of their family has tried to be helpful in the past but now keep their distance. There was a DUI three months ago and the person has to go to court for this in the near future. Despite all this, the person has never been involved in any treatment for depression and has taken no steps to get any help for their alcohol use. What can you say using these stages to help them think about taking steps to get help?

Stage 1 Rationale: Given the focus on punishment, we should think about any relevant potential or actual punishment. Life is, in one sense, punishing this person for not getting the help they need. The costs of lost employment and lost family relationships are all forms of natural punishment. These penalties have probably been happening for some time, but it may be helpful to point out that they are likely to continue and even get worse until the person takes steps to change things—steps to get help. More concretely, they are at risk for legal punishment when they go to court. Taking steps to seek help will be seen in a positive light by the judge.

Stage 2 Rationale: Given the focus on what they want, we should ask them about what is important to them right now. Mental illness and substance use are almost always a threat to what people want, but they are often reluctant to see that clearly.

If this person wants something specific like a better-paying job, it will be our task to point out how getting help with their depression and substance use will make that more likely to happen. If this person wants something broader, like a renewed sense of self-respect or to be close to their parents again, then our task is to explain how getting help likely will result in that.

Stage 3 Rationale: Given the focus on what their peers are doing, we want to help them see what other people their age are doing and what other people do in terms of help seeking. If they have a lot of friends who also drink heavily, it is often helpful to point out that their current friends may drink heavily but that most people their age do not. Every mental illness and substance use disorder is experienced by a relatively small percentage of the population at any one time. It can be very helpful to point out that only 10 percent of the population has had an alcohol use disorder in the past year or that 10 percent met criteria for major depression in the past year. It can also be useful to point out that most people who struggle with the problems will eventually seek help (80 percent for an alcohol use disorder, more than 80 percent for major depression). The key is to emphasize that other people get help and recover, and so should they.

Stage 4 Rationale: Given the focus on authority and social order, we should refer to authorities in their lives: parents, bosses, religious leaders, medical doctors, scientists, the law, rules at work, and so on. What do these authorities suggest about their current behavior? What would these authorities say about how they should be dealing with their problems? Wouldn't they support the idea of taking responsible action to get help to change the problem? We may also want to pull in healthcare authorities and guidelines. There are clear treatment guidelines for addressing each specific mental illness, and taking action to seek help is virtually always the first guideline.

Stage 5 Rationale: Given the focus on what is best for the most people, we should think about the costs of these untreated problems for the person, their family, their friends, their employers, and their community. The burden of untreated mental health problems is borne by a much larger group of people than our clients typically recognize. Employers often lose a great deal of money from lost time at work, poor performance, and loss of employees. Families lose the functioning of a key member, resulting in poorer support for everyone, and loss of parenting and partners. Friendships by definition involve mutual support, and untreated mental illness usually undermines our ability to think about and address the needs of our friends. The cost to the person may not persuade them to seek help, but pointing out the overall costs to family, friends, neighbors, employers, and the community may change their decision.

Stage 6 Rationale: Given the focus on universal principles, we want to ask our client about the key values they live by. People will often identify a range of values. Our task is to help them identify how their untreated depression and alcohol use is a barrier to their ability to live out those values. If they say love is their ultimate value, it is not hard to point out that not taking active steps to get rid of depression is not consistent with love for oneself or for those around who need our love. If they say service to others, we can point out how untreated depression makes us feel less interested and less able to focus on the needs of others. If they say honesty, we can point to the inherent problem in not honestly addressing a problem when we recognize it. There are a wide variety of responses, but with some forethought you'll be able to highlight some discrepancy here.

In summary, these six stages of moral reasoning can help us create rationales that will prompt others to change their decisions about seeking help. All these stages are relevant to all of us, and so I would suggest thinking about them for every client. I try to address all of them and refer to all of them during conversations when possible.

You may find it tempting to push your clients with these arguments. Remember the guidelines from other chapters about the impact of heavy pressure on others. It will be more effective to have these arguments handy for the opportunities to raise them, but avoid heavy pressure.

CHAPTER 15

STRATEGIES FOR WORKING WITH FAMILY, FRIENDS, AND OTHERS

Involvement from family and friends varies widely in our decisions to seek professional or peer support help. When they are involved, family members and friends typically play an important role, making the difference between someone getting the help they need or suffering for years before getting help. There is also evidence that, for some people, family and friends actually function as a barrier to getting help, and they do better without their involvement! Because family and friends are usually involved in some way, it is better to be aware of their involvement and to influence it in a way that helps your client.

FAMILY

Married people tend to have better mental health than single people. Part of the reason is that partners are typically involved in identifying and interpreting early symptoms of stress and mental illness, thinking through whether treatment should be sought, and ensuring it is when appropriate (Reczek, Thomeer, Gebhardt-Kram & Umberson, 2020). We may think about treatment decisions as individual (Moloney, 2017), but we almost always involve family members, either as sources of information or in helping us think through decisions (Reczek, Thomeer, Gebhardt-Kram & Umberson, 2020).

Family members often help us identify whether symptoms are "serious" or not, and whether they can be managed without formal help. Once we decide to seek treatment, family members often help us set up and attend appointments, and help with follow-up. Given these facts, it is clear that working with family, friends, and others is a key part of engagement work.
So, we need to embrace this important aspect of the work.

STRATEGIES FOR WORKING WITH FAMILY MEMBERS

1. **Attend to "Choice" and "Privacy" Factors.** Be aware of the rules related to your ability to talk to family members, and abide by those rules. Clients typically have to give us permission to include family members in discussions and decisions. We need their permission if we are even to acknowledge anything about our client's involvement or need for treatment. Even when we have permission to include them, family members can almost never overrule decisions for their relatives. Work with your supervisor and organization to be sure you are attending to these important rules *before* you talk to any family members.

2. **Be Clear About Who Your Client Is and Who You Are "Working" For.** Your legal obligation is to work in the interest, and under the guidance, of your client. Avoid situations in which you are or appear to be serving family members instead of your client. This can be particularly tricky for some clients and some families, so work closely with your supervisor anytime this becomes even a little challenging. I routinely ask my clients for permission to talk with family members and to provide any information or service for family members. Your client should almost never be surprised by anything you are saying or doing with their family.

3. **Provide Basic Education About Illness, Care, and Recovery.** Education is so helpful for family members. We forget that they need to learn about these topics if they are to effectively support their relative. Just providing basic information will often greatly improve their involvement in the situation.

4. **Help Them Understand How They Can Be Most Helpful.** I remind family members that they will be most helpful when they are "working alongside" the client, instead of trying to control or dominate the situation. They can have a very positive influence by expressing their concern and by offering help once the client decides what they want. Family members may need encouragement to not force their relative into decisions against their will.

5. **Look for Ways to Connect Family Members with Other Family Members for Peer Support.** They will benefit from getting to know other people in the same situation. Look for ways to create this opportunity, either

through family education groups, family support groups, or referrals to existing self-help groups for family members like Al-Anon, NAMI Family-to-Family, or Parents Anonymous.

6. **Help Them Recognize and Address Any Negative Impacts on Them.** For example, being a concerned family member is often stressful. Caregiving for family members with dementia is so stressful that it has been found to shorten the average caregiver's lifespan. Aiding family members who are stressed can help them minimize any negative impacts on themselves while allowing them to be supportive to your client for a longer period of time.

WHEN FAMILY IS A BARRIER TO TREATMENT ENTRY

This is unfortunately more common than we might guess. I was involved in developing a new intervention for clients who were unemployed because of a mental illness and who wanted to go back to work. The intervention was designed to educate them on how to go back to work while building their confidence that they could work successfully. It worked very well—almost all participants left feeling excited and confident about getting a job. They then went home, and the majority were talked out of going back to work by their family members. When we asked the family members why they dissuaded their relative from getting a job, their answers were surprising but quite logical. They said (1) they were afraid their relative would fail like they had done in the past, and then would "get sick again"; (2) they were afraid that going back to work would create stress for their relative and that would also lead to relapse; (3) they and other family members had "adjusted" to their relative not working, and they felt that changing that again would be stressful for the family; and (4) they reported being concerned that their relative would lose disability income if they went back to work.

These are common concerns by family members. We need to anticipate and address them proactively to ensure families are supportive of treatment and don't become barriers. Common strategies include:

1. Include family members in discussions early about treatment.

2. Provide education about treatment, outcomes (including possible negative outcomes), and likely costs.

3. Help them understand the recovery model and how it relates to taking risks.

4. Build their confidence and hope about the likelihood and benefits of recovery.

5. Give them a chance to talk about their fears and concerns.

6. Ensure they know about supports and services that are available if there are relapses or negative outcomes.

7. Give them a chance to talk about the changes that families face when clients improve; open discussion of these feelings will help everyone make better decisions.

8. Know and educate them about the rules for disability compensation and other supports that can function as disincentives for recovery. There are a growing number of programs to protect these supports while the person recovers, but you will need to know about them and share them with the family.

9. Normalize and destigmatize treatment and mental illness. Address stigma in the family when it is obvious. Again, offering opportunities for family members to receive peer support from other families can be an effective way to address stigma.

FRIENDS

Friends are less likely to be directly involved in treatment decisions, but in some cases they are very influential. Like family members, friends can have a positive or negative impact on treatment decisions—and usually for the same reasons. I find it important to ask about what friends are involved to ensure I don't get surprised by overlooking a key voice in the discussions. Again, the client has to provide permission for us to talk with the friend and for the friend to have any formal contact with us. When they do, I often use the same strategies listed above for family members.

HEALTHCARE PROVIDERS

Other healthcare providers are often very influential on clients' decisions about treatments. They can be key to encouraging clients to be involved in needed treatments, and they can also be barriers. Guidelines for working with healthcare providers are a little different from those for families:

1. **Attend to Guidelines About Privacy.** As with family members, you will want to attend to issues of permission and choice. You will likely need permission from your client to talk with their other providers. Consultation with other providers is subject to a range of rules, and so you'll want to work with your supervisor and organization to ensure you know those rules and are following them.

2. **If You Have Permission, You May Want to Talk with Other Key Providers About Treatment-Entry Issues.** In most cases, this will not be particularly helpful, but I do look for situations in which an ambivalent client has a provider whom they highly trust and who would likely support treatment entry. In those cases, I will reach out to that provider for a conversation.

3. **Connect Around Your Shared Interest in the Welfare of Your Client.** Clinicians usually have an inherent concern for their clients. Use this to remind them that you have the same agenda and that their assistance will help their client.

4. **Respect the Time Constraints of the Provider.** They are often busy and may not have time to talk. If you ignore those pressures, they are less likely to talk with you now and in the future.

5. **Respect the Freedom of Providers to Not Be Involved.** They may not feel willing or able to talk to you or to be involved in discussions of other treatment decisions. Don't take it personally—it may reflect a range of issues.

6. **Provide Basic Education About the Clinical Needs You See and the Treatments Available.** Don't assume that because they are a clinician, they know everything about all forms of treatment or that they know about the needs of the client. Be willing to provide a brief summary of the needs and opportunities you see.

7. **Remind Them of the Power of Provider Recommendations.** Patients are surprisingly compliant with recommendations from their providers, and

particularly from their primary care doctor. Reminding other providers of their power and influence can help them decide to get involved.

CHAPTER 16

ADVOCATING FOR OUTREACH AND ENGAGEMENT SERVICES

WHY THIS IS NEEDED

More than half of adults with mental healthcare needs in the United States are not participating in any treatment, and when they do, there is a median delay of eleven years before they enter needed care. While there is evidence that the proportion receiving treatment has increased slightly over the past twenty years, there is still a huge gap between what is needed and what is being addressed (Kessler et al., 2005; Wang, Berglund, Olfson & Kessler, 2004; Wang et al., 2005b).

Healthcare organizations have tended to be fairly passive in the face of this long-standing pattern of extended delays in needed treatment entry. Their traditional stance has been to wait until patients come to them. They act unconcerned about people who aren't seeking their help. The problem with this stance is that it results in more suffering and more cost to those individuals, their families, their employers, the broader community, and ultimately the healthcare industry.

You may be fortunate to work for an organization that understands the value of putting time and resources into outreach and engagement services. It is more likely, however, that you work for an organization that doesn't fully understand the importance of these services or that has not taken the need seriously. For many of you, doing this type of work will require advocacy within your own organization to help them understand the importance of this work and to fully support and resource it.

THINKING ABOUT ADVOCACY

Advocacy is defined as the act of recommending, supporting, pleading for, arguing for, or bringing pressure to bear in the support of a cause or proposal. Advocacy is a central function of Peer Support Specialists, reflecting the fact that they have a unique and invaluable perspective on the needs of clients and potential clients. By any measure that I am aware of, outreach and engagement to people with untreated mental illness is under-resourced and underrecognized and advocacy is needed to correct that.

Modern healthcare in the US typically keeps providers focused on trying to care for those in their offices while they try to stay afloat financially. This is a short-term, and shortsighted strategy that results in lost opportunities for the providers and for their clients. These organizations need to change a great deal with respect to this issue, and you have a perfect perspective in your work to help them do that.

COMMON EXCUSES FOR NOT SUPPORTING OUTREACH AND ENGAGEMENT

1. **"It's not in our mission."** The reality is that outreach and engagement are part of their mission. The Veterans Health Administration (VHA) is the largest integrated healthcare system in the United States. Their stated mission is to "honor America's Veterans by providing exceptional health care that improves their health and well-being." The stated mission of Kaiser Permanente, one of the largest healthcare providers, is "to provide high-quality, affordable health care services and to improve the health of our members and the communities we serve." The Joint Commission's stated mission is "to continuously improve health care for the public, in collaboration with other stakeholders, by evaluating health care organizations and inspiring them to excel in providing safe and effective care of the highest quality and value."

   All focus not only on those currently receiving care but also the larger community. Prevention and addressing unmet needs among members and future members clearly fit in the intention of these organizations. Encouraging participation in peer support enhances clinical outcomes and thus member health. Recent efforts by the VHA to provide care to unenrolled veterans reflect their growing conviction they are responsible for unenrolled and potential future "customers" with unmet healthcare needs (Ruiz, Burgo-Black, Hunt, Miller & Spelman, 2023).

2. **"It can't be done."** It is being done. In other areas of healthcare, it is current practice to reach out to at-risk

populations and engage them in needed care. This happens through programs like community-based screening for hepatitis or HIV. There are school-based screening programs for depression and for early identification and engagement of psychosis. These programs have been shown to be both clinically effective and cost-effective (Ledesma, Buti, Domínguez-Hernández, Casado & Esteban, 2020; Moore, Dowdy, Hinton, DiStefano & Greer, 2022).

3. **"We can't handle the patients we already have."** Our current challenge in keeping up with workload reflects the results of letting people wait years before they enter care—they are sicker and need more labor-intensive care. Strategic planning must involve discussions about how new approaches will improve the current flow of work. Clearly, early intervention in mental health would reduce the work demands represented by clients who currently come for care after years of untreated illness.

4. **"There is no real benefit to getting to people early."** We don't consistently calculate the cost of delayed care, including the cost to the healthcare provider and to the family. A number of clear examples where this is being done (psychosis, dementia, HIV, prenatal care, cancer, work injuries) provide models of how early intervention benefits everyone (Angelo, Vittorio, Anna & Antonio, 2011; Barnett, Lewis, Blackwell & Taylor, 2014).

5. **"We don't know how to do this."** Again, this is already happening for specific medical and mental health conditions. We do know how to do this.

6. **"We can't get reimbursed for this."** It is true that many outreach activities do not produce income in the

way that clinical care does. They do, however, produce income for healthcare organizations by bringing new clients into care. Many services that healthcare employees provide do not directly generate income, including healthcare administration, but they still add value in a way that eventually results in income.

ARGUING FROM THE QUALITY PERSPECTIVE

The Joint Commission (JC), Committee on Accreditation of Rehabilitation Facilities (CARF), and other credentialing bodies provide regular reviews of the quality of care that healthcare organizations are providing. Prevention, early treatment, and enhanced quality of care are all within the scope of these organizations.

Quality eventually points back to the ultimate value of improving the lives of patients and the community. When I have described the choice between outreach and engagement of people with untreated, maybe unrecognized mental illness versus waiting for years until they have accrued the negative impact of untreated illness, I have never found a quality assurance advocate to disagree that the outreach and engagement strategy is more consistent with the mission of quality healthcare.

ARGUING FROM THE FINANCIAL PERSPECTIVE

Evaluation of financial outcomes of any new program requires that we first ask whom the financial outcome is for. Is this for the healthcare organization? For the community? For the government?

I believe we can argue successfully from any of those perspectives:

1. For the community: Mental illness is a major source of disability and cost to our communities. Some of the largest costs are found in lost work potential and lost functioning in families. Untreated mental illness is associated with all these costs.

2. For the government: The costs to our communities, to employers, and families have a direct impact on the government. Untreated mental illness is also associated with additional governmental costs in terms of disruptive behavior that impacts the law enforcement and legal systems, supports for social services organizations, and the risk of very expensive services for those with extreme needs, such as homeless adults.

3. For healthcare organizations: Prevention and early intervention are designed to preclude the need for more expensive, more intensive interventions for people whose untreated illnesses have become more debilitating. Shifting the demands of care from late-stage intensive mental healthcare to early outpatient intervention will result in more people being served, and with less labor-intensive services.

As noted, there are existing early screening and engagement efforts for medical and for mental health problems that have been shown to be cost-effective. We need more research on ways to do this with other mental illnesses, such as depression and anxiety.

TALKING TO HEALTHCARE ADMINISTRATORS

Healthcare administrators are routinely involved in strategic planning for their organizations. They will be key voices in any discussion about incorporating early outreach and engagement programming. They will need to hear a rationale from a quality assurance perspective and from a financial perspective before they are likely to support this programming. I also find that communicating a set of arguments based on Kohlberg's theory of moral reasoning (see chapter 14) is often helpful for this key group of stakeholders. Here are some possible arguments to consider.

Stage 1: Focus on Obedience and Avoidance of Punishment. Currently, there are no clear "punishments" or penalties for not embracing this preventive approach to mental health programming. However, the field has embraced this approach for a growing number of disorders (e.g. psychosis), and this trend will certainly continue. Embracing this effort now will mean you will be ahead of the game and so won't have to work later to avoid the likely penalties that will be implemented in the future.

Stage 2: Focus on Self-Interest—What Do I Want? Implementing early engagement and treatment programs will result in a number of potential rewards for any healthcare administrator. It is innovative and will garner attention from other organizations and other administrators. It shows a clear focus on the welfare of the community and of clients, and so will bolster recognition of your commitment to the community. It will be very well received by the Joint Commission and CARF, and so will benefit your future reviews. It will result in more clients for your organization, and less expensive care, which should benefit your organization financially.

Stage 3: Focus on What the Majority of People Think Is Right—Conformity with Expectations. As can be seen in the growing number of published articles and clinical guidelines for this work, the clinical community increasingly sees early intervention efforts as an essential part of healthcare, and of a public health perspective. If we do not join this effort to embrace early engagement in the larger group of mental illnesses, we will be behind the current international and national norms in healthcare.

Stage 4: Focus on Authority and Social Order—What Do the Authorities and Social Order Require? Prevention of illness and of disability is one of the newest growing trends in evidence-based healthcare. We already have guidelines for early engagement services for some mental health conditions, such as psychosis. These broader efforts are in the pipeline and will be required of us in the future via clinical guidelines.

Stage 5: Focus on the "Social Contract," the Balance of Rules and Individual Rights in the Service of the Larger Group. Early diagnosis and treatment engagement are in the best interest of our clients and the larger community. They will reduce the costs that we all pay for untreated mental illness. We are not overruling individual rights, because clients still have the ultimate decision of whether to enter care.

Stage 6: Focus on Universal Ethical Principles Such as Love and Truth. Early engagement of adults with untreated mental illness is the right thing to do. As a healthcare organization, we need to pursue what is best for our current clients, our future clients, and our communities, even when clients don't see the need or when their illnesses undermine that need. Because of our commitment to their welfare, we need to develop this programming.

You may also want to use anecdotes about people who benefited from early treatment and people who waited for years to enter treatment, and the costs to those people, their families, the community, and healthcare providers. These will not be difficult to develop - you already know some of these people. Like recovery stories, these individual examples can be very persuasive for many stakeholders.

TALKING TO CLINICIANS

Clinical providers have a fairly different perspective than healthcare administrators. They spend most of their time meeting directly with clients and almost always have a deep concern for the welfare of their clients. This concern can be the key factor in gaining their support for early engagement efforts in your organization.

Because of their clinical work, clinicians typically are very aware of the cost of delayed care. They see it all the time. They may need help in framing what they see as the result on untreated mental illness, but that is not difficult to do.

Because of their typically busy work schedules, they may be likely to be concerned that new engagement programs may result in them being overwhelmed with new clients. You will need to help them see that this is a change in the entire process of care, resulting in more people seeking early care and fewer people seeking the intensive care needed to address problems that went untreated for years.

Clinicians **know they don't** typically have direct power in decisions about developing or expanding outreach and engagement services. They may need to be reminded that if they support these efforts, their support will carry a great deal of weight with the administrators who do.

TALKING TO COMMUNITY STAKEHOLDERS

At times, community stakeholders can have a key voice in decisions about outreach services. Hospital administrators are often interacting with them and are concerned about their expectations.

Community stakeholders represent a number of groups, including employers, colleges/universities, families, law enforcement, and the courts, who bear the cost of untreated mental illness. All these groups have learned to accept that some employees, students, family members, and citizens will have untreated mental illness and so will behave in ways that create significant problems for them. They may need help in realizing that this does not have to be the case. You may need to do significant work with this group to help them envision how early intervention could reduce the problems they see and that often involve them. Once they see this, you may have to help them bring their voice to the discussions where they can support these efforts.

PART III: CUSTOMIZING YOUR APPROACH BY THE TYPE OF NEED AND CLIENT

CHAPTER 17

SUBSTANCE USE DISORDERS

Each of the chapters in part III is designed to give you basic statistics to help you better understand the situation your client is in. The statistics are also selected to help your clients better calculate the costs of their illness and the likely costs if they continue to avoid treatment. Success rates for common treatments will also help them in their decision.

NATURE OF THE ILLNESS

Substance use disorders are among the most common mental health conditions, affecting about 29 percent of adults over their lifetime (Grant et al., 2016) and about 10 percent in any one twelve-month period. Individuals who meet criteria for these disorders have "impaired" control over how much they use substances and continue to use those substances despite serious negative impacts on their lives.

SUMMARY OF THE COMMON COURSE OF ILLNESS

Mild disorders are common in early adulthood, and often stop at that point. More chronic problems continue past early adulthood and often require formal treatment. Over time, substance use typically results in secondary medical, social, and behavioral problems that can motivate individuals to stop using. They can also bring the substance use to the attention of medical healthcare providers who may try to encourage the person to stop using for the sake of their health.

RATES OF TREATMENT ENTRY

Alcohol

Treatment entry for alcohol use disorder is relatively slow, if it happens at all. The limited available data suggest that by the time someone has had an alcohol use disorder for five years, about 30 percent will have participated in some form of treatment. It takes eighteen years before half will have participated in any treatment, and by thirty years, about 70 percent will have participated. About 20 to 30 percent will continue to have an active alcohol use disorder without ever entering treatment.

Because of the high rate of people with untreated alcohol use disorder, there has been a lot of research on how people most often get identified and enter treatment. Primary care providers do see these people but will often miss the problem unless they use a formal screening technique. A simple screening tool like the WHO AUDIT or AUDIT-C greatly increases the number of people who get a diagnosis and a referral to treatment.

Many people will be first diagnosed when they enter treatment for some of the serious medical problems that result from chronic alcohol use, including liver disease or gastrointestinal problems. Some will be diagnosed when they enter treatment for other mental health conditions, such as depression, anxiety, or marital and family problems. Others will be diagnosed after they get in trouble with the law for behavioral problems arising from their use of alcohol.

Other Substances

Like alcohol, participation in treatment for other drug use (stimulants like cocaine, opioids like heroin, hallucinogens like PCP, sedatives like Xanax, as well as marijuana, inhalants and tobacco) disorders is relatively low compared to anxiety and mood disorders. Studies do show that adults with a drug use disorder are significantly more likely to participate in treatment than those with an alcohol use disorder (Blanco et al., 2015; Olfson, Blanco, Wall, Liu & Grant, 2019).

THE PROCESS OF RECOVERY

Alcohol

Spontaneous Recovery and Relapse: Estimates for how many people with an alcohol use disorder will recover without any treatment are difficult to establish, but researchers have concluded that it is not uncommon and that more people probably recover without formal treatment than with treatment (Price, Risk, Spitznagel, 2001; Tucker, Chandler & Witkiewitz, 2020).

When researchers follow people over years, it is clear that when spontaneous recovery happens, it occurs typically after multiple unsuccessful efforts to quit. People who recover without treatment point to pressure from family members, health concerns, and support from other people who do not drink. When they are compared with people who recover through treatment and/or AA, those who use no supportive services are less likely to maintain stable abstinence (Moos & Moos, 2007).

For those who do establish recovery, relapse is common. This pattern of relapse has led some to suggest that a broader focus for treatment success is needed, including the notion of "treatment careers" (Dennis, Scott, Funk & Foss, 2005). This perspective focuses on long-term patterns of treatment participation and abstinence instead of short-term success. This can be helpful to your clients who need a broader focus to see their progress.

Mortality and Common Health Implications: Alcohol use disorders result in significantly shortened lives. One large study in Europe found that they are associated with an average decrease in life expectancy of twenty-four to twenty-eight years (Westman et al., 2015). This dramatic number reflects the reality that chronic alcohol use is very hard on our bodies, taking a serious toll over the years. Mortality statistics are important for clients to know and can help them better calculate the cost and benefit of treatment.

Common health problems resulting from extended alcohol use include diabetes mellitus, coronary heart disease, cancer, cardiovascular disease, and liver and pancreas disease, among others (Rehm et al., 2010). Nonnatural forms of death associated with alcohol use include suicide and accidental death (Borges, Bagge, Cherpitel, Conner, Orozco & Rossow, 2017; Chikritzhs & Livingston, 2021). These potential costs should also be included in your client's decision.

Treatment Success Rates: Large studies that average the success rates over many treatments suggest that about 40 to 60 percent of participants stay abstinent following participation in an evidence-based treatment (Timko, Moos, Finney & Lesar, 2000). When AA or other 12-step support is integrated into the treatment, success rates are higher and subsequent reliance on healthcare services is reduced (Humphreys & Moos, 2007).

Clients often underestimate the success rates of treatments, and these statistics can help them make good decisions about whether to enter care.

Other Substances

Spontaneous Recovery and Relapse: Estimates for how many people with a drug use disorder will recover without any treatment range widely, though evidence points to the rates being significantly higher than those with alcohol use disorders, and more common than recovery resulting from formal treatment (Price, Risk & Spitznagel, 2001). Even people who don't enter treatment and don't recover often reduce their drug use, either because of the problems it causes or because of health concerns, and/or the urging of family and friends (Walters, 2000).

Mortality and Common Health Implications: Drug use disorders result in significantly shortened lives (Charlson et al., 2015), with estimates of a decrease in life expectancy across all illicit drugs of four years for the average man and two for the average woman (Glei & Preston, 2020). If we focus on specific substances, those using opioids are particularly at risk for early death and injury, with an overall risk of premature death that is fifteen times the risk of average adults (Degenhardt et al., 2011).

A wide range of health problems result from extended drug use, depending on the substances being used. For example, use of any substance over time raises the risk of death or injury by overdose, accidental injuries and violence, cardiovascular disease, liver disease, a range of mental disorders including psychosis, suicide, and bloodborne bacterial and viral infections, notably HIV, hepatitis B, and hepatitis C (Charlson et al., 2015).

Treatment Success Rates: Large studies that average the success rates over many treatments suggest that about 30 to 60 percent of participants stay abstinent after completion of formal treatment (Dutra et al., 2008).

BRIEF SUMMARY OF THE MOST COMMON TREATMENTS

Brief interventions administered in primary care can be effective for mild alcohol use disorders. Primary care is also a place where routine screening can help identify people with more severe forms of this disorder and refer them for more intensive treatment.

Medications: The most common pharmacological tools used with substance use disorders are those used to reduce cravings and desire for use. These are growing in popularity. Other medications are used during withdrawal to help manage that process.

Psychotherapies: Talking therapies are common and often effective. Common targeted psychotherapies include CBT, contingency management, motivational interviewing, couples and family interventions, and combinations of these interventions. Relapse prevention is another common talking intervention designed to extend periods of abstinence.

Peer Support/Self-Help Groups: These groups are among the most common interventions used. Alcoholics Anonymous is the largest self-help organization and has an extensive array of groups around the world. There are substance-specific versions of AA, including Narcotics Anonymous, Marijuana Anonymous, Cocaine Anonymous, Nicotine Anonymous, and Crystal Meth Anonymous. Other organizations use a different format than AA, including Moderation Management, SMART Recovery, LifeRing Secular Recovery, Women for Sobriety, and Secular Organizations for Sobriety. Finally, there are offshoot organizations providing peer support for family members, including Al-Anon and Alateen.

Inpatient, Residential, Intensive Outpatient, and Traditional Outpatient Services: These services are also frequently used as a means to increase the intensity of treatment and/or create space for treatment that is separate from environmental opportunities to use.

Harm-Reduction Strategies: The goal of harm-reduction interventions is to reduce both the individual and societal harms of alcohol and substance use through knowledge-based interventions. A secondary goal is to encourage treatment entry for those who will not participate in an abstinence-only treatment.

For alcohol use, harm-reduction interventions often focus on education, peer support, and strategies for reducing risk of alcohol use. Common interventions for illegal drugs, especially opioids and the central nervous system stimulants, include (1) opioid substitution treatment; (2) needle and syringe programs; (3) supervised drug-consumption facilities; (4) drug overdose prevention; (5) outreach, peer education, and health promotion; (6) testing, vaccination, and treatment of drug-related infectious diseases; and (7) interventions for stimulant users.

Research evidence supports the idea that harm-reduction strategies do result in reduced risk of health problems and risk of accidental injury and death (Witkiewitz et al., 2020; Charlet & Heinz, 2017).

COMMON FACTORS IN TREATMENT ENTRY

The symptoms of substance use disorders reflect a pattern of choosing to use substances over choosing to attend to one's own health and other life responsibilities. The pattern of slow treatment entry fits with the notion that substance use alters our judgments about taking care of ourselves, and so the illness itself is a key barrier to treatment entry.

Substance use over time often creates medical problems that can help move treatment entry forward. Worries about health can cause people to seek help. Illnesses can bring the related substance use to the attention of doctors and other medical providers who can then talk with their patients about the importance of treatment.

Family members are often concerned about substance use and can be a key voice in encouraging or even leveraging treatment entry. Overall, family involvement in treatment and in treatment entry is associated with better outcomes. When they are not involved, it is often due to clinicians not involving them and sometimes the family choosing not to be involved (Easson, Giacco, Dirik & Priebe, 2014). At the same time, family members can be barriers to treatment entry, particularly when they are also using.

Harm reduction is a treatment strategy that has opened doors to a large number of people who are not willing to participate in abstinence-only services.

CHAPTER 18

PTSD AND OTHER TRAUMA AND STRESS-RELATED DISORDERS

NATURE OF THE ILLNESS

The *Diagnostic and Statistical Manual of Mental Disorders (DSM-5)* identifies a traumatic event as "exposure to actual or threatened death, serious injury, or sexual violation, as directly experiencing traumatic events, learning of the traumatic events experienced by a close family member or close friend, or repeated exposure to aversive details of the traumatic events." About 70 percent of the population will experience this type of event in their lifetime, though only a minority (about 6 percent) will develop symptoms sufficient for a diagnosis of PTSD.

The symptoms of PTSD have been revised in *DSM-5* to four clusters, including intrusion (such as flashbacks or intrusive memories), avoidance (such as avoidance of people or places that trigger memories of the trauma), negative alteration in cognition and mood associated with the traumatic event, and marked alterations in arousal and reactivity associated with traumatic events (such as being chronically alert for danger).

SUMMARY OF THE COMMON COURSE OF ILLNESS

Exposure to traumatic events is surprisingly common, with the largest surveys suggesting 30 percent of people are exposed to more than three events in their lifetime (Benjet et al., 2016). Most people who experience trauma do not develop PTSD, but exposure to more trauma raises the risk of developing it. Some of the common risk groups for PTSD include combat veterans and people working in jobs where they are at risk for seeing traumatic events (police and other first responders, prison guards, emergency room doctors, etc.). Women are more likely to develop PTSD after a trauma than men.

There is a lot of variation in how PTSD develops over time. For most people, symptoms develop soon after the trauma, though in a minority (<5 percent), they can develop after a delay of a year or more. Once people develop symptoms, some get better relatively quickly, while others have difficulty for years. In one key study (Santiago et al., 2013), about a third of those who developed PTSD got better without any treatment, usually within three months. About 40 percent developed a chronic course that lasted years.

RATES OF TREATMENT ENTRY

It is difficult to find data on the typical time to first treatment entry for PTSD. The data available (Fikretoglu, Brunet, Guay & Pedlar, 2007) suggests that a significant number of people never enter treatment, and those that do often do so after time. Seeking help is more likely among adults with more severe symptoms, and when symptoms interfere with work or family life.

THE PROCESS OF RECOVERY

Spontaneous Recovery and Relapse: In at least one study, a third of those meeting criteria for PTSD recovered without treatment. Relapse in PTSD is poorly understood and so the research offers limited information (Berge, Hagen & Øveraas Halvorsen, 2020). There is more data describing how PTSD can often trigger relapse in substance use disorders.

Mortality and Common Health Implications: Chronic PTSD is associated with significant health problems and reduced lifespan (Roberts, Kubzansky, Chibnik, Rimm & Koenen, 2020).

Trauma and PTSD are associated with increased risk of physical and mental health problems. The risk of cardiovascular problems, diabetes, and stroke increases with trauma exposure. The most common risk for mental health is depression, with about half of all adults with PTSD having significant depression. Other mental health risks are for substance use disorders, anxiety disorders, suicidal ideation, and suicide. Chronic PTSD is associated with decline in functioning in work, school, and family relationships and friendships.

Treatment Success Rates: For those entering treatment, success rates overall are around 60 to 70 percent, though they can differ by treatment (Bradley, Greene, Russ, Dutra & Westen, 2005; Watkins, Sprang & Rothbaum, 2018). About 30 percent have been identified as "treatment resistant," meaning that they participated in treatment but have not experienced significant success. There is some evidence that receiving treatment in specialty mental healthcare may have better outcomes than in primary care.

BRIEF SUMMARY OF THE MOST COMMON TREATMENTS

Medications: Medications can be helpful to manage PTSD symptoms, though there is a general agreement that some medications, such as benzodiazepines or other sedative hypnotic medications, can cause symptoms to worsen over time (Schrader & Ross, 2021).

Psychotherapy: Most talking therapies have a specific focus on talking about the trauma. The most common talking therapies designed specifically for PTSD include:

- Cognitive processing therapy (CPT)

- Prolonged exposure therapy (PE)

- Eye movement, desensitization, and restructuring (EMDR)

Because these therapies involve talking about the trauma, engagement can be a challenge (Gallegos, Streltzov & Stecker, 2016).

Inpatient, Residential, Intensive Outpatient, and Psychosocial Rehabilitation Services: These services may be used, depending on the severity of the PTSD and the need for intensive treatment. Rehabilitation services including interventions like supported employment have been found to be effective (Davis et al., 2012).

COMMON FACTORS IN TREATMENT ENTRY

PTSD symptoms include the tendency to avoid anything that reminds the person of the traumatic event. For many, that avoidance includes talking about the trauma or the need for treatment. Even when they are able to talk about the need for treatment, adults with PTSD often feel anxiety as they get closer to participating in treatment. For this reason, most of the treatments involve teaching the client ways to reduce their anxiety, which helps them get through the experience of treatment.

Drop out is common across treatments. A recent review found the average across all talking therapies to be 16 percent, with those therapies that focus on talking about the trauma being higher—up to 30 percent (Lewis, Roberts, Gibson & Bisson, 2020).

CHAPTER 19

MOOD DISORDERS

NATURE OF THE ILLNESS

Mood disorders involve marked disruptions in emotion, with severe lows (called *depression*) and/or highs (called *mania*). This group of disorders includes major depressive disorder, bipolar disorder, and the less common disorders of cyclothymia, hypomania, disruptive mood dysregulation disorder, persistent depressive disorder, and premenstrual dysphoric disorder.

Major depression is a common disorder marked by the presence of five or more of the following nine symptoms: sad mood, feelings of guilt, decreased energy levels, decreased concentration, decreased appetite, decrease in pleasurable activities, either increased or decreased physical activity, insomnia, and recurrent suicidal ideation/suicide attempt or self-harm. These symptoms have to be present for at least two weeks.

Bipolar disorder, also a common disorder, includes periods of depression, but is also marked by periods of symptoms of mania—elevated mood with three or more of the following symptoms: racing thoughts, increased grandiosity, a diminished need for sleep, distractibility, increased/pressured speech, increased goal-directed activity, and reckless behavior. These symptoms have to be present for at least one week or be so severe that they require hospitalization.

SUMMARY OF THE COMMON COURSE OF ILLNESS

Major Depression

About 5 to 10 percent of adults will experience major depression in any given year, with women being twice as likely as men to develop depression. Between 30 and 50 percent of adults will experience significant depression in their lifetime. Researchers have concluded that about half of significant depressions will go away and not recur, while the other half will likely recur and become a problem over time (Lorenzo-Luaces, 2015).

Bipolar Disorder

About 1 to 2 percent of adults will have symptoms of bipolar disorder in any given year. This is generally seen as a chronic illness that is often misunderstood and misdiagnosed in younger adults, in part because the symptoms typically ebb and flow. Unfortunately, symptoms usually recur over time, bringing long-term challenges to functioning at work and in relationships.

RATES OF TREATMENT ENTRY

Major Depression

Treatment entry for depression is slow, with 35 percent of patients entering treatment within two years of symptoms appearing and 50 percent within eight years. About 80 percent will eventually seek treatment, but it can take thirty or more years, with a full 20 percent never seeking treatment (Kessler, Olfson & Berglund, 1998; Thornicroft et al., 2017).

Bipolar Disorder

Specific data on time to first treatment is not easy to find. It is clear that there are high levels of undiagnosed and untreated young adults with bipolar disorder (Charney et al., 2003). Delays in diagnosis are lengthy (mean 12.5 years), clinically important, and associated with problems in social functioning (Matza, Rajagopalan, Thompson & De Lissovov, 2005), as well as an increased risk of lifetime suicidality (Nery-Fernandes et al., 2012). Indeed, the delay in diagnosis risks young people receiving inappropriate treatment, which may worsen the condition. Delays in diagnosis and treatment are costly, and early treatment is associated with better outcomes (Joyce, Thompson & Marwaha, 2016).

THE PROCESS OF RECOVERY

Major Depression

Spontaneous Recovery and Relapse: Many people do recover from depression without treatment. In one study, 23 percent recovered within three months, 32 percent within six months, and 53 percent within twelve months (Whiteford, Harris, McKeon, Baxter, Pennell, Barendregt & Wang, 2013). Unfortunately, depression often recurs, and so spontaneous recovery may actually be temporary.

Mortality and Common Health Implications: Major depression is associated with a reduced lifespan, though the actual cause of that reduction is not clear. Major depression is associated with suicide risk and unhealthy behaviors like smoking. It is also associated with poor response to medical problems, like not seeking help, which can lead to greater illness.

Major depression is also associated with a higher risk of cardiovascular disorder, cancer, and neurodegenerative disorders (Berk et al., 2023). Having those medical illnesses can cause depression, but research suggests that depression can raise our risk of these illnesses as well.

Treatment Success Rates: Fifty to seventy percent of adults starting a first medication for major depression will have a positive response. Thirty to seventy percent will have a positive response to psychotherapy, with evidence of better outcomes with the combination of medication and talking therapy.

Bipolar Disorder
Spontaneous Recovery and Relapse: Bipolar disorder includes a pattern of symptoms that come and go over time. This is not considered spontaneous recovery, as the ebb and flow are part of the illness. It is typically viewed as a chronic illness that can be managed. Relapses are common even among adults with well-managed symptoms, with one study finding about 50 percent of adults relapsing within one year and 75 percent within five years. Psychotherapies have been found to reduce relapse rates (Scott, Colom & Victa, 2007).

Mortality and Common Health Implications: Bipolar disorder is associated with a significant reduction in lifespan. This appears to be related both to risk of unnatural causes of death (like suicide) and to natural medical causes that are found at higher rates in those with this disorder (Biazus et al., 2023). Bipolar disorder is also associated with increased risk of cardiovascular disease, diabetes, pulmonary disease, infectious disease, and musculoskeletal conditions like low back pain (McIntyre et al., 2006).

Treatment Success Rates: Early diagnosis and treatment have been shown to result in better long-term outcomes. Treatment success over time also appears closely related to the degree to which there is a strong relationship between the client and the clinician, as this illness requires ongoing collaboration between patient and provider.

BRIEF SUMMARY OF THE MOST COMMON TREATMENTS

Major Depression

Medications: Medications are often used to treat major depression, with a range of different types of medications potentially helping. It is not uncommon for adults to have to try more than one medication before they find one that works for them. Antidepressants often take some time to work, and so clients need to be patient to see if any specific medication will work for them and what, if any, side effects may occur.

Psychotherapy: Talk therapy is common and often effective, and a wide range of therapies are used for depression. Some of the most common that have the strongest research support include cognitive behavioral therapy and interpersonal psychotherapy for depression.

Somatic Therapies: You may find clients who are considering participating in electroconvulsive therapy (ECT), transcranial magnetic stimulation (TMS), vagal nerve stimulation (VNS), and deep brain stimulation (DBS). These therapies are increasingly used for treatment-resistant depression.

Peer Support Groups: Groups for depression are available but are less well known. National organizations such as the Depression and Bipolar Support Alliance (DBSA), Anxiety & Depression Association of America (ADAA), and Depressed Anonymous provide some of the most focused support groups.

Bipolar Disorder

Medications: Medications are commonly used to treat bipolar disorder, including mood stabilizers such as lithium or valproic acid and atypical antipsychotics such as risperidone, olanzapine, quetiapine, ziprasidone, or aripiprazole.

Psychotherapy and Case Management: These are also common and usually focus on helping the person manage their symptoms and address any functional challenges, such as work and school.

Education: Common interventions include education for family members, as well as other psychosocial interventions to support functioning. Severe symptoms can require hospitalization and may result in involvement with the law.

Somatic Therapies: There is good evidence for the use of ECT when symptoms are severe and other treatments have not worked. TMS, VNS, and DBS have been used, but the research support is still evolving.

Peer Support Groups: Groups for adults with bipolar disorder include those available for depression (DBSA, ADAA, and Depressed Anonymous). NAMI peer support groups and family-to-family groups may also be helpful.

COMMON FACTORS IN TREATMENT ENTRY

Major Depression

Symptoms of depression represent a serious barrier to seeking help. Feelings of hopelessness and helplessness undercut the actions needed to take the step of getting help and the patience and persistence needed to continue seeking it until effective treatments are found. Symptoms of guilt and low self-esteem can also contribute to ambivalence about seeking help. Finally, some adults with depression experience significant problems initiating any new actions, and so asking for help is commonly delayed.

Bipolar Disorder

The confusing nature of the symptoms in early bipolar disorder represent a serious barrier to help seeking. Clients may ask for help, but help for what? Clinicians can inaccurately diagnose this disorder as a substance use disorder, a personality disorder, or a number of other things that involve treatments that have no benefit for bipolar disorder.

At times, people find some of the symptoms of bipolar disorder to be positive. In particular, mild levels of mania are often associated with feelings of importance, empowerment, and energy. I have worked with clients who are ambivalent about treatment when it means they may not feel that way again.

The cyclical nature of the symptoms in mood disorders also represents a barrier to help seeking. Just as people start to think about getting help, their symptoms may disappear. Hope of getting better without treatment can lead people to wait a very long time before they decide that they need to take action.

The proliferation of early identification and treatment programs has resulted in greater interest among clinicians in early diagnosis and referral. If you can find an early-identification team in your area, they can be a valuable partner in helping these clients get treatment.

CHAPTER 20

ANXIETY DISORDERS

NATURE OF THE ILLNESS

Anxiety disorders, as a group, are the most prevalent psychiatric disorders. They include excessive anxiety and worry, but they come in fairly different forms. Specific phobias are the most common form, at around 10 percent of the population, followed by panic disorder (PD; 6.0 percent), social anxiety disorder (SAD; 2.7 percent), and generalized anxiety disorder (GAD; 2.2 percent). Generally, women are one and a half to two times as likely to develop an anxiety disorder as men.

SUMMARY OF THE COMMON COURSE OF ILLNESS

Anxiety disorders are among the earliest mental illnesses to appear, with a median age of eleven (Kessler et al., 2005). Even with treatment, anxiety disorders tend to be present over a long period of time and take ongoing efforts to manage their symptoms and limit their impact on functioning (Ramsawh, Raffa, Edelen, Rende & Keller, 2009; Schopman, Have, van Balkom, deFraff & Batelaan, 2021).

RATES OF TREATMENT ENTRY

Phobias have a low rate of treatment entry. Only about 20 percent of adults with a phobia enter treatment within the first ten years of the illness, and more than 50 percent never enter treatment.

Panic disorder, which is marked by more uncomfortable, disruptive, and unpredictable symptoms, is associated with much more rapid help seeking. More than 50 percent of adults with panic disorder enter treatment within one year, and only 10 percent never seek treatment. Generalized anxiety disorder (GAD) falls in the middle, with about 40 percent seeking treatment in the first year, 60 percent in the first ten years, and more than 90 percent eventually entering treatment (Kessler, Olfson & Berglund, 1998). There are very few studies of treatment entry for Social Anxiety Disorder (SAD). Those available suggest found that up to a third of adults with SAD have not entered any treatment, and that those who do, often are treated for comorbid conditions (Olfson et al., 2000).

THE PROCESS OF RECOVERY

Spontaneous Recovery and Relapse: Most anxiety disorders have low spontaneous recovery rates and significant risk of relapse (Wittchen, 1988).

Mortality and Common Health Implications: There is no evidence that anxiety disorders are associated with a shortened lifespan by themselves (Miloyan, Bulley, Bandeen-Roche, Eaton & Gonçalves-Bradley, 2016).

Anxiety disorders are more common in patients with chronic medical problems including cardiovascular disease, gastrointestinal disease, respiratory disease, migraine, chronic pain, and cancer, but it is not likely that anxiety causes these disorders. It is clear that anxiety disorders contribute to worse symptoms and functional impairment in many chronic medical conditions such as asthma, cardiovascular disease, and diabetes and increase risk for the incidence and disease progression in others such as cardiovascular disease (Kroenke, Spitzer, Williams, Monahan & Löwe, 2007).

Treatment Success Rates: Phobias have among the best success rates, ranging up to 80 to 90 percent (Wolitzky-Taylor, Horowitz, Powers & Telch, 2008).

Panic disorder success rates are also fairly encouraging, with about 75 percent of treatment participants showing benefits that last for years (Saeed & Bruce, 1998).

In SAD, success rates range widely but average around 50 percent for full recovery and 80 percent for at least partial recovery.

GAD rates are similar, with around 50 percent of treatment completers no longer meeting criteria for at least twelve months after completion.

BRIEF SUMMARY OF THE MOST COMMON TREATMENTS

Medications: Medications with established efficacy include selective serotonin reuptake inhibitors (SSRIs), as well as other antidepressants. Certain anticonvulsants and antipsychotics may be helpful.

Psychotherapy: Cognitive behavioral therapy (CBT) has been shown to have good success with PD, GAD, phobias, and SAD (Ziffra, 2021). Treatment for phobias has focused on exposing the patient to what they are anxious about, either through indirect or direct exposure. Success rates for exposure therapies are high, but the experience can be stressful and so it is not uncommon that patients avoid or drop out of them.

Peer Support/Self-Help Groups: People with anxiety disorders can benefit from peer support, though there are fewer self-help organizations that specifically target this group. The Anxiety & Depression Association of America (ADAA) is one exception. Other broader self-help organizations like NAMI or DBSA are often helpful places where people struggling with anxiety disorders can find support.

COMMON FACTORS IN TREATMENT ENTRY

We try to avoid things that make us anxious, and so patients may extend this to seeking treatment for anxiety disorders. Disorders that are particularly uncomfortable, like panic disorder, are associated with more rapid help seeking. Treatment entry rates for phobias and social anxiety are remarkably low.

Many people cope with anxiety disorders by avoiding the situations that make them anxious. This is likely a key reason for the low treatment entry rates for phobias, as people just avoid what they are afraid of. Similarly, SAD is common and often untreated, with many people simply avoiding social situations. This can be a costly strategy, given the impact on health and functioning. Efforts to encourage these individuals to enter treatment can have special benefits in terms of freeing them to live more active and more socially connected lives.

Families don't always notice the presence of anxiety disorders clearly, and so may need help and education seeing the opportunity for their relative to get treatments that help them feel and function better.

CHAPTER 21

PSYCHOSIS

NATURE OF THE ILLNESS

In clinical settings, the terms *psychosis* or *psychotic symptoms* refer to a problem in thinking or perception, most notably taking the form of delusions or hallucinations. They can occur in a wide range of disorders, including dementia, substance use, severe depression, and bipolar disorder. A *psychotic disorder* refers to a group of mental illnesses in which psychotic symptoms are prominent and meet specific diagnostic criteria for a disease. The psychotic disorders in the *DSM-5* are distinguished from one another mainly by their duration (e.g., six months or more for symptoms of schizophrenia and less than a month for a brief psychotic disorder).

The key symptoms may include things like fixed false beliefs (delusions, such as the belief that one is being poisoned), hallucinations (seeing or hearing things that are not real), disorganized thoughts represented by illogical and incoherent speech, and abnormal motor behavior, such as bizarre postures. Some of these symptoms may not be apparent to the casual observer, as they require the person to report them. The group that you may work most commonly with is those with schizophrenia, representing about 1 percent of the adult population.

SUMMARY OF THE COMMON COURSE OF ILLNESS

Schizophrenia and schizoaffective disorder most often begin in early adulthood. The course of these disorders typically varies over time, with periods of severe symptoms and other periods of relatively fewer symptoms. These disorders are generally associated with some of the highest degrees of disability in work and social life, though there is wide variation between individuals. People with psychotic disorders are at higher risk for complications like suicide, poor health and healthcare, substance abuse, and homelessness.

Recent research efforts suggest that early identification and treatment can result in significant improvement in long-term symptoms and their impact on functioning.

RATES OF TREATMENT ENTRY

Time to first treatment entry ranges from weeks to several years (Larsen, McGlashan & Moe, 1996). Factors supporting early treatment entry include the often-dramatic initial symptoms. Unfortunately, these same symptoms can be misinterpreted as resulting from other disorders like substance use, and so misdiagnosis and inappropriate treatment are common factors in the delay of early treatment. Involuntary hospitalization and contact with law enforcement can be part of early identification and treatment.

THE PROCESS OF RECOVERY

Spontaneous Recovery and Relapse: Spontaneous recovery is not common in disorders like schizophrenia and schizoaffective disorder (Salzer, Brusilovskiy & Townley, 2018). Brief psychosis can be the result of other conditions, and so spontaneous recovery from a brief psychosis is considered evidence of a different disorder (Fusar-Poli et al., 2016). In schizophrenia and schizoaffective disorder, relapse is common over time, and stress can be a precipitant of relapse.

Mortality and Common Health Implications: People diagnosed with schizophrenia live, on average, fifteen to twenty years less than nonaffected adults (Correll et al., 2022). Suicide and other nonnatural causes of death appear to be the biggest risk factor, but a range of illness and health factors, including the health impacts from antipsychotic medications, also contribute to this increased mortality (Marder et al., 2004).

Adults with schizophrenia are at higher risk for several illnesses, including diabetes, coronary heart disease, hypertension, and emphysema. The lifestyles of people with schizophrenia often include patterns of poor diet, obesity, smoking, and the use of alcohol and street drugs, which may explain part of these elevated risks. Some antipsychotic medications used to treat schizophrenia have been associated with weight gain, the onset of diabetes, and other significant health risks.

Treatment Success Rates: Traditionally, clinicians have not been optimistic about treatment success for psychotic disorders. More recently, interest in recovery and in measuring improvement in this group has provided evidence for more optimism. In one study that followed adults with a first episode of psychosis for two years, 50 percent had remission of their symptoms, 25 percent had remission of their functioning, and 20 percent had both (Wunderink, Sytema, Nienhuis & Wiersma, 2009). Studies that followed people over a longer period of time found that about 50 percent were found to have at least some symptom and functional remission by the twenty-year mark (Peralta et al., 2022; Morgan et al., 2014).

BRIEF SUMMARY OF THE MOST COMMON TREATMENTS

Medication: Medication is the most common form of treatment for psychotic disorders, with over twenty different antipsychotic medications in wide use. They are often effective in reducing or eliminating some but not all symptoms, but they often have side effects that are concerning to clients (e.g. dry mouth, dizziness, weight gain). It is also common that multiple medications must be tried before the right one is found, testing the persistence of the client.

Psychotherapy and Case Management: These are typically focused on helping the person understand their illness, manage their symptoms, reduce their stress, and build their social functioning. CBT for psychosis is an increasingly popular targeted form of therapy.

Psychosocial Rehabilitation Interventions: A number of well-studied programs focus on building functioning and community integration, including clubhouses, intensive rehabilitation programming, supported employment/education, and cognitive rehabilitation.

Somatic Therapies: Brain-stimulation techniques, such as electroconvulsive therapy (ECT), transcranial magnetic stimulation (TMS), transcranial direct-current stimulation (tDCS), and deep brain stimulation (DBS), have been used for psychotic disorders.

Peer Support/Self-Help Groups: Group options are also commonly used, including NAMI peer support and family groups, Recovery International, Wellness Recovery Action Plan (WRAP) support groups, and Schizophrenics Anonymous.

COMMON FACTORS IN TREATMENT ENTRY

Symptoms of psychotic disorders typically involve impaired judgment and self-awareness—two key elements required for effective help seeking. Anxiety, paranoia, and misunderstanding of others' behavior are all common and undermine the client's willingness to reach out for professional help or peer support. They may also have difficulty initiating action or communicating clearly, which can make seeking treatment difficult. Finally, a great deal of stigma is associated with psychotic disorders. No one wants to think of themselves as having such a serious mental illness. This can create an incentive for individuals and their families to avoid facing the situation honestly, hoping that something else is causing the symptoms.

Family and friends often take an active role in supporting treatment entry, as they can see from the typically dramatic early symptoms that the person is in need of treatment. Their involvement is often needed in obtaining that help, as the person may have very low recognition of any need for care. The behavioral symptoms of these disorders may increase the likelihood that police and the court systems may be involved in treatment entry.

Research shows that early treatment for psychotic disorders has significant lasting benefits for the person, which has resulted in the rapid growth of "Early Psychosis" programs. These programs can be good resources and partners for helping people struggling with an untreated psychosis to enter needed treatment.

CHAPTER 22

SUICIDAL IDEATION

NATURE OF THE ILLNESS

Suicidal ideation is common, affecting about 4 to 6 percent of the adult population in any one year, and 11 to 20 percent at some point in their lifetime (Castillejos, Huertas, Martin & Moreno Kuestner, 2021; Liu, Bettis & Burke, 2020). Suicidal thoughts are much more common than successful suicide, with one large study finding that less than 1 percent of adults experiencing suicidal thoughts take their own lives (de Winter, Meijer, Kool & de Groot, 2023).

Despite that, death by suicide is too common. Each year there are more than 700,000 deaths due to suicide worldwide and almost 50,000 deaths in the United States (Ferrari et al., 2014; Vigo et al., 2016). Suicidal ideation and deaths impact people across all age groups—children, adolescents, and older adults. Older adults have a relatively elevated risk of suicide and suicidal ideation (Stone, Jones & Mack, 2021). Women are more likely to have suicidal ideation and to make suicide attempts, while men are more likely to die by suicide (Moitra et al., 2021).

The risk of suicide and suicidal ideation is elevated in mental illness, with particularly clear elevations in adults with mood disorders like depression and bipolar disorder, substance use disorders, and schizophrenia (Li, Page, Martin & Taylor, 2011; Esang & Ahmed, 2018).

Given the association between suicidal ideation and mental illness, data suggesting that large numbers of adults with suicidal ideation are not involved in mental health treatment is concerning. In a large European study, more than 40 percent of adults with suicidal ideation were not involved in mental health treatment. In a study in the US, almost 70 percent of veterans with suicidal ideation were not involved in mental healthcare (Nichter et al., 2021).

SUMMARY OF THE COMMON COURSE OF ILLNESS

Suicidal ideation can vary widely in its course, with some people experiencing it briefly as part of a passing life or health crisis, while others can experience chronic long-term suicidal ideation (Have et al., 2009).

RATES OF TREATMENT ENTRY

We have limited data about the time to first treatment for suicidal ideation. We know that many people are not in treatment, suggesting that rapid treatment entry is not common. In a large World Health Organization study of people who had tried to take their lives in the previous year, most had not sought help in the subsequent twelve months (Bruffaerts et al., 2011). When asked why they had not sought help, more than half said they did not need any help, and another large subgroup said they wanted to take care of the issue themselves.

THE PROCESS OF RECOVERY

Spontaneous Recovery and Relapse: For many people, suicidal ideation occurs in response to a specific crisis, and when the situation resolves and/or time goes by, they no longer think about taking their own lives. Relapse of suicidal ideation is often seen as part of relapse of other mental illnesses. Hospitalization and more serious suicidal behavior are associated with a higher risk of the subsequent relapse of suicidal ideation (Suárez-Pinilla et al., 2020).

Mortality and Common Health Implications: Suicidal ideation is associated with a shortened lifespan. This appears to be related to the risk of suicide and the risks associated with mental health conditions (Shiner, Riblet, Westgate, Young-Xu & Watts, 2016). Most of the available data documents that suicidal ideation is found more often in adults with mental health conditions and adults in crises related to serious medical conditions. Suicidal ideation is a correlate and is caused by those conditions, and is not seen as the cause.

Treatment Success Rates: Evidence-based psychotherapies have been found to reduce suicidal ideation by more than 50 percent (Schneider, Chen, Lungu & Grasso, 2020).

BRIEF SUMMARY OF THE MOST COMMON TREATMENTS

There have been a number of treatment strategies for suicidal ideation. In many cases, the focus is on treating the common mental health condition that is seen as "causing" the suicidal ideation. Another common strategy is to manage the risk of suicide with monitoring, efforts to restrict the means of suicide, and, when necessary, hospitalization. More recently, there has been growing interest in interventions that directly target suicidal ideation.

Medications: Besides treating depression and other underlying mental health conditions with medications, there has been growing interest in the use of the medication ketamine as a targeted treatment for suicidal ideation. One recent study found that ketamine had a 60 percent success rate (Can et al., 2021), though there are reasons to be cautious as more studies are needed (Witt et al., 2020).

Psychotherapy: Talking therapies such as dialectical behavior therapy (DBT) and cognitive therapy for suicide prevention (CT-SP) have been found to reduce suicidal ideation and suicide attempts by more than 50 percent (Méndez-Bustos, Calati, Rubio-Ramirez, Olie, Courtet & Lopez-Castroman, 2019). These treatments target depression and borderline personality disorder but can be used in a broader group of people. Specific forms of therapy targeting suicidal ideation are under development in the Department of Veterans Affairs and are likely to be disseminated in the future.

Psychosocial Rehabilitation: Interventions to enhance the client's social and work life have been increasingly seen as tools for reducing suicidal ideation and risk of suicide (Stevenson et al., 2023). They represent preventive strategies that fall under the rubric of "building a life worth living."

COMMON FACTORS IN TREATMENT ENTRY

It is clear from large research studies that many people don't seek help for suicidal ideation because they don't see it as a problem that requires it, or they want to address it themselves. This is likely a result of several factors, including denial of the need for help, the impact of stigma associated with suicidal ideation, and in some cases, the fact that feeling suicidal may be a temporary response to stressful events that may go away without treatment. When they do engage in care, they are at risk for fragmented care that can increase risk (Strike, Rhodes, Bergmans & Links, 2006). Given the potential cost of not seeking help, the healthcare system has taken a very aggressive stance toward taking action when suicidal ideation is noted. This recent approach appears to be showing success in terms of declines in deaths by suicide.

CHAPTER 23

"PERSONALITY DISORDERS"

NATURE OF THE ILLNESS

There is a great deal of disagreement about the topic of personality disorders. Clinical providers use this term to refer to a group of people who have significant struggles in relationships and work and who can benefit from treatment. According to the American Psychiatric Association (APA), a personality disorder is a mental health condition where people have a lifelong pattern of seeing themselves and reacting to others in ways that cause problems. Personality varies widely, but when a persistent pattern of personality functioning creates significant problems for that person or those around them, this is referred to as a "personality disorder." These patterns must create problems in how the person relates to others, affecting their family life, social activities, work and school performance, and overall quality of life. These disorders have different patterns, including narcissistic, paranoid, avoidant, and antisocial styles of interacting.

SUMMARY OF THE COMMON COURSE OF ILLNESS

Personality disorders are by definition long-term patterns of behavior. They tend to be present early in life and to persist over many years. Some people change behaviors over time to improve their functioning, but often the underlying pattern continues to be present to some degree.

RATES OF TREATMENT ENTRY

Data on specific entry rates by personality disorder are not as available as for other disorders. We do know that people rarely enter treatment to specifically address their personality disorder. More commonly, they find their way into treatment in order to deal with the problems created by it. Many find their way into treatment through marital therapy because of conflict with their partner. Others may get involved because of feelings of depression or anxiety and the related functional problems. Still others enter treatment through the courts or because of getting in trouble at work.

Treatment entry varies among the types of personality disorders and seems most closely related to the likelihood that (1) the person is distressed (depressed or anxious) about their functioning problems, or (2) others are pressuring them to enter treatment because of the problems they create for others. For example, a large percentage of adults diagnosed with borderline personality disorder participate in treatment, often over years (Zanarini, Frankenburg, Reich & Fitzmaurice, 2015), probably because of the common symptoms of anxiety and depression they experience. Adults meeting criteria for antisocial personality disorder don't tend to feel anxious or depressed often, and rarely enter treatment for that disorder. However, they are at higher risk for substance use disorders and thus are often in treatment to address substance use.

Once in treatment, the patterns of participation vary by the personality style. Adults with antisocial personality disorder tend to have difficulty with rules and authority, and are at high risk for dropping out of treatment early. Those with dependent personality disorder often stay in treatment for extended periods of time, given their tendency to become dependent on their providers (Simonelli & Parolin, 2020).

THE PROCESS OF RECOVERY

Spontaneous Recovery and Relapse: By definition, personality disorders represent stable patterns of functioning over years. Spontaneous recovery is not common, though there is some data suggesting that rates of personality disorder decline with age (Holzer & Vaughn, 2017) and, specifically, that some adults with disorders like antisocial and borderline personality disorder will tend to become less symptomatic as they get toward middle and late adulthood (Zanarini, Frankenburg, Reich & Fitzmaurice, 2012). In one study with a particularly long follow-up (forty-five years), about 20 percent of adults with antisocial personality disorder no longer met criteria over time (Black, Baumgard & Bell, 1995).

Mortality and Common Health Implications: Having a personality disorder is associated with an average reduction of lifespan of fifteen to eighteen years (Fok et al., 2012; Björkenstam, Björkenstam, Holm, Gerdin & Ekselius, 2015). These disorders are associated with increased risk of natural death and nonnatural death like suicide. Personality disorders are associated with elevated risk for a number of medical conditions, including cardiovascular disease, arthritis, obesity, chronic pain, and sleep disturbance. Depending on the disorder, they are also associated with a range of mental health conditions, including depression, anxiety, and substance use (Dixon-Gordon, Whalen, Layden & Chapman, 2015; Frankenburg & Zanarini, 2006).

Treatment Success Rates: Some personality disorders have few or no research studies evaluating treatment successes, and so it is difficult to suggest success rates. Borderline personality disorder has been the focus of the most treatment evaluations, and the results are encouraging, with success rates for therapies like dialectical behavior therapy (DBT) falling in the 30 to 50 percent range (Gradman, Thompson & Gallagher-Thompson, 2013). There are growing applications of psychotherapies for disorders like dependent, avoidant, and obsessive-compulsive personality disorder, with less consistent but still encouraging results.

BRIEF SUMMARY OF THE MOST COMMON TREATMENTS

Medication: Medication can be used to address secondary mental health problems like depression, anxiety, or thought disorder.

Psychotherapy: This is the most common intervention provided to specifically address the personality disorder. The most common form of therapy is DBT, which was developed to specifically address symptoms of borderline personality disorder. Other psychosocial interventions have been tried, including cognitive behavioral therapy, behavior therapy, and social skills training (Dixon-Gordon, Turner & Chapman, 2011).

COMMON FACTORS IN TREATMENT ENTRY

Personality patterns that result in problems working with other people are the hallmark of personality disorders. These patterns often impact help seeking, and so the disorders are part of why these individuals often do not enter treatment in a timely way. Poor insight, poor collaboration with others, and disruptive behaviors all can slow the process of getting the right treatment and participating in a way that results in a good outcome. Family and friends are often key allies that can help these adults enter needed care. Employers and the legal system can also provide some incentive for getting into treatment. Given the stability of these disorders, it is important to think of long-term patterns of treatment participation.

CHAPTER 24

HELP SEEKING AND DIVERSITY

This chapter is designed to give you useful information about the relationship between your clients' background variables and barriers to engagement in mental healthcare and self-help groups. You want to be alert to factors that may suggest that your client is more or less likely to seek out needed help. This information will be valuable for understanding your client and may also be useful to share with your client.

For example, you might be working with a client who grew up in a rural part of your state. They would clearly benefit from entering mental health treatment, but they have not done so. The fact that their rural background is a significant risk factor for delayed use of mental health services should give you a warning that this client may be resistant to considering care. The strong values of independence and self-reliance, particularly common in people from rural backgrounds, have been identified as key barriers to treatment entry (Fischer et al., 2016). Knowing this can give you a clue as to topics to discuss with this particular client. You might say something like, "I understand that you are not particularly interested in talking with your doctor about getting help for your depression. Would it be OK if I shared some information that might be relevant? There is research that shows that people like yourself who grew up in a rural area really value solving your own problems—much more so than other people in the rest of the country. I have great respect for that value. But in some situations, it can actually create a danger for you. Dealing with serious depression is challenging—not something you want to do by yourself usually. You wouldn't want to try to fix your own diabetes or cancer without working with your doctor. Why would you try to fix a complex problem like clinical depression without working with your doctor?"

That line of discussion may or may not help your client decide to seek help. It is likely, however, to help you quickly move to some of the key issues impacting their decision. That is the goal of this chapter: to help you address the key issues relatively quickly by knowing some of the relationships between engagement and background issues.

GENDER, GENDER IDENTITY, AND SEXUAL ORIENTATION

In general, women use more healthcare services and are more willing to seek help than men (Bertakis, Azari, Helms, Callahan & Robbins, 2000). They are also more likely to recognize a need for care (Olsson, Hensing, Burström & Löve, 2021). This is particularly true when it comes to mental health services, with women being more likely to see a need and to participate in mental healthcare (Rens, Michielson, Dom, Remmen & Van den Broeck, 2022). Men are less likely to enter care, and when they do, they are more likely to drop out early (Reneses, Munoz & Lopez-Ibor, 2009). This may be due in part to how they view healthcare and mental healthcare—with evidence from research suggesting that men are more likely to equate mental healthcare with weakness (Wendt & Shafer, 2016).

The acronym *LGBTQ* combines references to sexual orientation with gender identity. *Sexual orientation* refers to the "emotional, romantic, sexual or affectional attraction to another person." *Gender identity* is a **person**'s self-perception as a man or woman. *Transgender* refers to people whose gender identity is at odds with the gender they were assigned at birth according to their sex and physiological characteristics. *Sexual identity* refers to the cognitive and emotional meaning one attaches to expressions of sexuality, which includes romantic, emotional, and social preferences (Moagi, van der Wath, Jiyane & Rikhotso, 2021).

LGBTQ populations are more likely to experience mental health symptoms—primarily depression, suicidal ideation, and suicidal behaviors (Mustanski, Garofalo & Emerson, 2010). These differences start in childhood and early adolescence and continue through adulthood (McDermott et al., 2021). LGBTQ adults are more likely to report unmet mental health treatment needs (Steele et al., 2017), and so help with treatment entry is clearly needed. There have been efforts to create specialized mental health services adapted for the LGBTQ population. This appears to be present in around 20 percent of the mental health clinics and reflects reports by LGBTQ clients who state that mental health clinicians often need additional education in this area. Stigma, discrimination, and the complex psychological issues related to sexual orientation and gender identity make treatment engagement a complex challenge for many adults. Well-trained Peer Support Specialists and outreach workers who can provide supportive education and collaboration around treatment entry, and particularly entry into clinical programs knowledgeable about working with LGBTQ populations, would clearly be valuable in working with this group.

AGE AND EDUCATION

Among adults, younger age is associated with more unmet need for mental healthcare (Baiden, Den Dunnen & Fallon, 2017; Yang, Roman-Urrestarazu, McKee & Brayne, 2019). Once they enter care, younger adults are more likely to drop out. I have found that it often takes years for adults to understand their own mental health challenges and how to effectively work with providers and self-help groups. Younger adults often have not yet learned the value of getting and using help, and so are less likely to do so.

Having a college education or higher is associated with a higher rate of recognizing a need for care and a higher rate of using needed mental healthcare, relative to those with a high school education level (Olsson, Hensing, Burström & Löve, 2021). Once in care, people with a college education or higher are less likely to drop out.

FINANCIAL STATUS

Income and overall financial resources are related to having health insurance, and insurance is directly related to use of mental health services (Walker, Cummings, Hockenberry & Druss, 2015). It appears that the perception of need and the willingness to participate in care is a larger predictor of use than having resources for treatment (Steele, Dewa & Lee, 2007). For example, in a large study of college students who had access to full healthcare resources, most of those who needed mental healthcare did not access it. When asked why, most said they did not see a need or were unaware of services. Even when financial resources for care were controlled, having a lower socioeconomic background was still predictive of not seeking care (Eisenberg, Gollust, Golberstein & Hefner, 2007).

RACE AND ETHNICITY

The relationship between healthcare, healthcare providers, and racial/ethnic subgroups in the US is a complicated one. There has been a great deal of research on this topic, and almost all studies have found that race and ethnicity have strong relationships with whether people use healthcare and particularly mental healthcare.

For example, there are studies that suggest that African American adults are more likely to use mental health services relative to white non-Hispanic adults, and are more likely to be hospitalized for a psychiatric disorder. At the same time, African Americans report higher rates of distrust of mental health providers and have lower levels of satisfaction with care when they receive it (Henderson et al., 2015). This is likely related to negative experiences with the healthcare system but may be related to broader experiences and distrust. There is also a higher degree of stigma for mental illness among African Americans, which is likely an additional barrier (Evans-Lacko, Henderson & Thornicroft, 2013).

For Hispanic adults, particularly for those from an immigrant background, there is a tendency to see a need for mental healthcare less often and to underutilize mental health services even when they do see a need (Bridges, de Arellano, Rheingold, Danielson & Silcott, 2010).

For Asian American clients, there is again a similar pattern of reporting less need for mental healthcare, and when they do see a need, they participate in care at lower rates than white non-Hispanic clients (Yang, Rodgers, Lee & Lê Cook, 2020). When you are working with clients from nonwhite backgrounds, be aware that seeking help from healthcare providers, and specifically mental health providers, may have complex personal meanings to them. You may want to help them talk about those meanings and to consider how they should or should not be included in their decision to get help.

Native Americans and Alaskan Natives are at a significantly higher risk of mental illness than the rest of the US population, with about 50 percent of Native Americans meeting criteria for a mental illness in the past year. Risk of substance use disorders and PTSD is particularly elevated (Beals et al., 2005). When it comes to seeking treatment, Native American and Alaskan Native women are more likely to seek out services and to participate in those services than men (Brave Heart et al., 2016).

Native Hawaiians and Pacific Islanders are a diverse group that includes a variety of subgroups. As a group, they have been found to have lower rates of substance use than other US citizens. Where there is a need for mental health treatment, the limited research data available suggests they are less likely to participate in treatment, either by choice or because of internal or external barriers (Wyatt, Ung, Park, Kwon & Trinh-Shevrin, 2015).

The relationship of race/ethnicity and healthcare is a very important one—one you want to know more about. I would encourage you to pursue additional training in this area so that you can work more effectively with the variety of clients you are likely to face.

RURAL VS. URBAN

Rural adults are less likely to participate in mental health treatment, and when they do, it is less likely to be specialized mental healthcare and less likely to be the more effective evidence-based forms of care (Hauenstein et al., 2006). This appears to be due to a number of situational factors, including less access to mental health providers and to current mental health programming in rural areas. It is also due to the values and perceptions common among rural adults. For example, one study found that having a high value of "self-reliance," which is very common in adults living in rural areas, was the single largest barrier to mental health treatment entry (Fischer et al., 2016).

MARITAL STATUS

Being married is predictive of reporting lesser unmet need for mental healthcare (Yang, Roman-Urrestarazu, McKee & Brayne, 2019). This is likely related to the broader finding that married individuals tend to have better health, live longer, and use healthcare more actively (Dupre, Beck & Meadows, 2009).

There is some evidence that in heterosexual marriages, women may tend to take on the role of "health expert" and "emotional expert," while men may be more likely to ignore their own and their wives' health and mental health problems (Reczek, Thomeer, Gebhardt-Kram & Umberson, 2020). If you are working with married men, and particularly those who value traditional gender roles, you will want to look for that tendency to not see needs, and to defer to their spouse for decisions about seeking help.

There are also important examples of when being married is not an advantage. In one study, married veterans had slower entry into treatment for alcohol dependence (Kirchner, Booth, Owen, Lancaster & Smith, 2000). In another study, it was only happily married adults who had the health and healthcare advantage, with unhappily married adults having no significant difference in health from unmarried adults (Lawrence, Rogers, Zajacova & Wadsworth, 2019).

VETERAN STATUS

Because of factors such as military selection, healthy lifestyle, and psychosocial factors predictive of who enlists in the military, veterans tend to have significant advantages over their civilian counterparts when it comes to physical health, mental health, academic and vocational success, and lifespan (Sullivan-Baca, Rehman & Haneef, 2023). Given the stressful experiences they face in the military, it is not surprising that veterans who have been deployed to combat zones have been found to have a higher rate of mental illness relative to those who have not been deployed and age-matched civilians (Hoglund & Schwartz, 2014). Elevated risk of PTSD and of suicidal ideation and suicide have drawn particular focus recently.

Data showing that younger veterans are less likely to delay entry into mental health treatment than their civilian counterparts or veterans who served before 9/11 (Goldberg et al., 2019) is encouraging and may reflect more active engagement efforts by the VA. Unfortunately, two-thirds of veterans are not enrolled in VA healthcare, and they have a significantly higher rate of untreated mental illness (Nichter et al., 2021).

Common barriers veterans face with regard to mental health treatment entry and help seeking include stigma, the military culture of stoicism and self-reliance, characteristics of combat exposure and different war zone deployments, healthcare access issues, and lack of understanding by civilian providers (Randles & Finnegan, 2021). The transition between military and civilian life can be a significant challenge that can create mental health difficulties and can represent a barrier to help seeking (Drebing et al., 2018).

LONELINESS AND SOCIAL ISOLATION

There is a great deal of current interest in social isolation and loneliness. Loneliness has been defined as "subjective social isolation," and has been associated with higher unmet need for healthcare, as well as higher health and mental health concerns and shorter lifespans (Byhoff et al., 2022; Holt-Lunstad, Smith, Baker, Harris & Stephenson, 2015).

General social support refers to perceived support or potential support from family, friends, and acquaintances. This broader type of support is negatively correlated with unmet need for mental healthcare (Baiden, Den Dunnen & Fallon, 2017).

Those who are socially isolated have more health concerns and more mental health needs. They also have been found to attend more meetings with their primary care providers (Cruwys, Wakefield, Sani, Dingle & Jetten, 2018), raising concerns among some researchers that they may be using healthcare meetings as a means of addressing unmet social needs. This has spawned the "social prescribing" movement in the UK, with some evidence that enhancing social support can cut down on the use of healthcare by those with low social support.

Each of your clients has a combination of background factors, current factors, and future potentials. With experience, you will gain greater insight into patterns within and between people. These patterns will help guide your efforts to help them make good treatment and peer support decisions for themselves and for those around them.

APPENDIX A: DEALING WITH CRITICAL SITUATIONS

As a Peer Specialist, you will be in situations where you may have to respond to a range of high-risk challenges. Knowing how to respond effectively is essential for all Peer Support Specialists, regardless of where you work and what your particular focus might be.

BROAD STRATEGIES

- Learn and follow the local guidelines for emergency responses at your organization. Talk about them with your supervisor so you are clear on all procedures before emergencies happen.

- Practice response procedures so you know them fully. Practice and preparation before an incident will ensure that you know how to respond well when a true emergency arises, and that you can do so while under stress.

- Alert others immediately when you find yourself in an emergency situation. Activate safety alert systems and notify other coworkers. Clinical providers have special training in dealing with clinical emergencies. Get them involved quickly and let them take the lead.

- Try to stay calm. Your ability to think clearly in an emergency will be critical for following through with an effective response.

- "First things first": Attend to immediate safety needs for yourself and those around you before placing all your attention elsewhere.

MAKING A 911 CALL

- Tell the operator what and where the emergency is.

- If someone is injured, tell the operator who is injured and the nature of the injury.

- If there are ongoing dangers in the area that could affect the responders, describe these for the operator.

- Give your name and phone number.

- Do *not* hang up until instructed to do so by the operator.

- After the call, notify your supervisor and/or other key personnel.

- Make sure someone meets the responders and guides them to the appropriate location.

- Do *not* move injured people unless it is absolutely necessary. If medical providers are available, let them decide whether to move anyone who has been hurt or administer other emergency first aid.

- Let the responders do their job once they arrive.

- Document your actions.

- After the event is over, talk with your supervisor and coworkers about how the response went and how it could be better next time.

SPECIFIC SITUATIONS:

A POTENTIALLY SUICIDAL CLIENT

Suicide is one of the top ten causes of death in the United States, and having a mental health or substance-use disorder is one of the most powerful predictors of suicide, suicide attempts, and suicidal thoughts. Peers are very likely to have contact with people who are suicidal, and so will want to seek out training and supervisor guidance on how to deal with this common and critical situation.

If you think someone may be suicidal, contact your supervisor or another available clinician as quickly as possible. Clinical providers often have significant training in assessing and responding to suicidal adults. Get them involved quickly and follow their guidance.

However, it's not always easy to know if a client is suicidal. Someone may need to ask the person for more information before it becomes clear that he or she is at risk. Talk with your supervisor about whether you should notify them immediately or first ask questions of the client directly on your own.

Watch for some of the following common warning signs:

- Talking about suicide.

- Getting the means to commit suicide.

- Being preoccupied with death.

- Withdrawing from social contact; wanting to be left alone.

- Feeling trapped or hopeless.

- Engaging in risky or self-destructive behaviors.

- Increasing substance use.

- Giving away belongings; getting affairs in order for death.

If you are going to speak with the client before seeking out a supervisor or other clinician, ask clear, simple questions:

- "Do you feel like giving up?"

- "Do you think a lot about dying?"

- "Have you been having thoughts about hurting yourself?"

- "Have you thought about how you might hurt yourself?"

- "Do you have the means of hurting yourself available to you?"

If you believe the client is actively suicidal:

- Do not leave the person alone—stay engaged with him or her.

- Get help as quickly as possible. Call a supervisor, 911, or the police, depending on how critical the situation is and who is immediately available to you.

- Keep the person engaged while help is coming.

- Encourage the person to get help.

- Offer to go with the person to get help.

- Be respectful of the person's feelings. Don't be judgmental or patronizing.

A POTENTIALLY HOMICIDAL OR VIOLENT CLIENT

Violence occurs in many work settings, including mental health settings. Training and preparation are critical for recognizing potential risks and preventing violent incidents.

If you think someone has the potential for violence in the near future, contact your supervisor or another available clinician immediately. Again, clinical providers typically have significant training in assessing and responding to potential violence. Get them involved quickly.

It's not always easy to recognize if someone has the potential to be violent in the near future. That's why it is important to take the following common precautions in all settings.

- If you work in a specific area, think about how to make the area safer. For example, make sure you have a way to leave safely if someone becomes threatening. Keep the space relatively uncluttered—eliminate items that someone could use to hurt you or others.

- Have ways to get help quickly, and know how to use them (e.g., panic buttons or alarms).

- Talk with coworkers and supervisors in your area about how you can work together to respond to a potentially violent situation.

- Know how to access security and police officials quickly. Talk with them about working together for safety.

- Request a formal assessment of safety by a licensed professional.

A SITUATION THAT INVOLVES POSSIBLE INTIMATE PARTNER VIOLENCE OR DOMESTIC ABUSE

Intimate partner violence (IPV) refers to physical or sexual violence, threats, or emotional abuse between people who have or have had an intimate relationship. Accurate data about IPV is difficult to collect, but at least 30 percent of women and 10 percent of men will experience IPV in their lifetimes.

Learn and follow the local guidelines for responding to these situations. Talk about them with your supervisor before you uncover actual situations and have to respond.

If you think you are working with someone involved in a violent relationship, or if you think it is likely there is violence, contact your supervisor or another available clinician as quickly as possible. As stated before, clinical providers often have significant training in identifying, assessing, and responding to violence.

It's often not easy to tell if someone is experiencing IPV, and many people are hesitant to talk about it. Watch for some of the most common warning signs that may identify victims of IPV:

- They appear overly afraid of or anxious to please their partner.

- They may talk about their partner's temper or possessive or controlling nature.

- They frequently make excuses for their partner's behavior and negative treatment of them.

- They may have a series of injuries, with vague or suspicious excuses.

- They may frequently miss work or school, again with vague

or suspicious excuses.

- They may be isolated from friends or family. They may rarely see others besides their partner.

The full range of warning signs of IPV, including signs that you are working with someone who may be violent with their partner, is beyond the scope of this pocket resource. Talk with your supervisor about learning more about this topic.

A SITUATION THAT INVOLVES POSSIBLE CHILD ABUSE

Child abuse is common, and can include physical, sexual, or emotional abuse or neglect. Estimates suggest that in the United States, five children die every day as a result of child abuse.

Learn and follow the local guidelines for responding to the discovery of child abuse. Talk about them with your supervisor before you uncover situations and have to respond.

Every state in the US has laws mandating professionals to report evidence of child abuse that they become aware of. Common mandated reporters include physicians, social workers, psychologists, counselors, teachers, and police. Peer Support Specialists and other people who may not be mandated to report child abuse can report it. Talk with your supervisor and local providers about how to handle situations in which you become aware of possible or likely child abuse. Again, clinical providers often have significant training in assessing and responding to child abuse. Get them involved quickly.

There is a wide range of warning signs of child abuse—a discussion of all of the signs is beyond the scope of this pocket resource. Talk with your supervisor to learn more.

A SITUATION THAT INVOLVES POSSIBLE ELDER ABUSE

Abuse of older adults is also surprisingly common and involves physical, sexual, or emotional abuse, as well as neglect or abandonment, or misuse of the older adult's money or property. Elder abuse can happen in families or in institutions that care for the elderly. Learn and follow the local and regional guidelines for responding to elder abuse. Talk about them with your supervisor before you uncover situations and have to respond.

Similar to child-abuse laws, there are regional laws mandating healthcare professionals to report elder abuse. If you think you are working with someone who might be a victim of elder abuse, contact your supervisor or another available clinician as quickly as possible. Watch for some of the most common warning signs that may identify victims of elder abuse:

- They may seem depressed or confused.

- They are losing weight for no reason.

- They have trouble sleeping.

- They act agitated or violent.

- They have become withdrawn.

- They stop taking part in activities enjoyed in the past.

- They have unexplained bruises, burns, or scars.

- They look messy; they may have unwashed hair or dirty clothes.

- They display signs of trauma (i.e., rocking back and forth).

- They develop bedsores or other preventable conditions.

APPENDIX B: USEFUL QUOTES RELATED TO HELP SEEKING

AVOIDING PROBLEMS

"Running away from your problems is a race you'll never win."
—*Anonymous*

"If you choose to not deal with an issue, then you give up your right of control over the issue and it will select the path of least resistance."
—*Susan Del Gatto*

"In a moment of decision, the best thing you can do is the right thing to do, the next best thing is the wrong thing, and the worst thing you can do is nothing."
—*Theodore Roosevelt*

"When you have to make a choice and don't make it, that in itself is a choice."
—*William James*

"Running away from any problem only increases the distance from the solution."
—*Anonymous*

"I realized that I only had two choices: I was either going to die or I was going to live, and which one did I want to do? And then I said those words, 'I'll get help,' or, 'I need help. I'll get help.' And my life turned around. Ridiculous for a human being to take 16 years to say, 'I need help.'"
—*Sir Elton John*

"The attempt to escape from pain, is what creates more pain."
—*Gabor Maté*

DENIAL

"Denial is the number one aspect of medicine. That's why people don't get check-ups."
—*Larry L. King*

"Denial is the lid on our emotional pressure cooker: the longer we leave it on, the more pressure we build up. Sooner or later, that pressure is bound to pop the lid, and we have an emotional crisis."
—*Susan Forward*

"Delay is the deadliest form of denial."
—*C. Northcote Parkinson*

DOING THE WORK

"A sum can be put right: but only by going back till you find the error and working it afresh from that point, never by simply going on."
—*C. S. Lewis, The Great Divorce*

"It's so much easier to suggest solutions when you don't know too much about the problem."
—*Malcolm Forbes*

"Think logically, and you have a chance to solve a problem. Reacting emotionally to it prolongs and worsens your dilemma."
—*Stewart Stafford*

"There is no magic wand that can solve our problems. The solution rests with our work and discipline."
—*Jose Eduardo dos Santos*

"Tackle the root cause not the effect."
—*Haresh Sippy*

"Any problem in the world always bows down to courage."
—*Sachin Ramdas Bharatiya*

"Most of the problems in life are because of two reasons: We act without thinking or we keep thinking without acting."
—*Zig Ziglar*

"A problem well stated is a problem half solved."
—*John Dewey*

FOCUS ON GOALS

"Don't be pushed by your problems. Be led by your dreams."
—*Ralph Waldo Emerson*

"There is no problem that you cannot solve if your focus is on solutions."
—*Nitin Namdeo*

"Be mindful of what you want, instead of what you don't want. Constantly focusing on the problem will not manifest the solution."
—*Anthon St. Maarten*

"Change is the law of life. And those who look only to the past or present are certain to miss the future. "
—*John F. Kennedy*

"Happiness is not the absence of problems, but the ability to deal with them."
—*Charles De Montesquieu*

OPTIMISIM

"Every strike brings me closer to the next home run."
—*Babe Ruth*

"Well, if it can be thought, it can be done, a problem can be overcome,"
—*E. A. Bucchianeri*

"Believe you can and you're halfway there."
—*Theodore Roosevelt*

There' s no use talking about the problem unless you talk about the solution.
—*Betty Williams*

"Every experience in your life is being orchestrated to teach you something you need to know to move forward."
—*Brian Tracy*

"Our greatest glory is not in never failing, but in rising up every time we fail."
—*Ralph Waldo Emerson*

PATIENCE AND PERSISTENCE

"A quick fix for a long-standing problem only works for the short term."
—*Dr. Jacinta Mpalyenkana, PhD, MBA*

"When solving problems, dig at the roots instead of just hacking at the leaves."
—*Anthony J. D'Angelo*

"A persistent problem, is an indication that you haven't given it GENUINE attention."
—*Mike Ssendikwanawa*

"Often just by taking action, by doing something about the situation you can relieve the stress and help correct the situation."
—*Catherine Pulsifer*

"The great thing in this world is not so much where you stand, as in what direction you are moving."
—*Oliver Wendell Holmes*

"Life is like riding a bicycle. To keep your balance, you must keep moving."
—*Albert Einstein*

CREATIVITY AND CHANGE

"We cannot solve our problems with the same level of thinking that created them."
—*Albert Einstein*

"If your only tool is a hammer then every problem looks like a nail."
—*Abraham Maslow*

"We are products of our past, but we don't have to be prisoners of it."
—*Rick Warren*

"Change, like healing, takes time."
—*Veronica Roth*

TAKE RESPONSIBILITY

God, grant me the serenity to accept the things I cannot change, the courage to change the things I can, and the wisdom to know the difference.
—*Serenity Prayer, Reinhold Neibuhr*

"We are taught you must blame your father, your sisters, your brothers, the school, the teachers—but never blame yourself. It's never your fault. But it's always your fault, because if you wanted to change, you're the one who has got to change."
—*Katharine Hepburn*

"Experience is not what happens to you, it is what you do with what happens to you."
—*Aldous Huxley*

"Anyone can stay the same. It takes courage to change."
—*John Assaraf*

ACCEPTANCE OF WHAT WE CAN'T CHANGE

"Incredible change happens in your life when you decide to take control of what you do have power over instead of craving control over what you don't."
—*Steve Maraboli*

"The best time to plant a tree was 20 years ago. The second-best time is now."
—*Chinese proverb*

"Change is inevitable in life. You can either resist it and potentially get run over by it, or you can choose to cooperate with it, adapt to it, and learn how to benefit from it. When you embrace change, you will begin to see it as an opportunity for growth."
—*Jack Canfield*

"Don't let the past steal your present."
—*Terri Guillemets*

TRYING TO CHANGE OTHER PEOPLE

"When people are ready to, they change. They never do it before then, and sometimes they die before they get around to it. You can't make them change if they don't want to, just like when they do want to, you can't stop them."
—Andy Warhol

"Don't expect to see a change if you don't make one."
—*Unknown*

"Never solve a problem for someone, instead, help them figure out how to solve it on their own. Otherwise, you destroy their adaptive competence."
—*Lord Robin*

Others

"Too often we give our children answers to remember rather than problems to solve."
—*Roger Lewin*

"Pull out the weeds, or make peace with the dandelions."
—*Frank Sonnenberg*

"A problem is a chance for you to do your best."
—*Duke Ellington*

REFERENCES

Angelo, C., Vittorio, M., Anna, M., & Antonio, P. (2011). Cost-effectiveness of treating first-episode psychosis: five-year follow-up results from an Italian early intervention programme. *Early Intervention in Psychiatry*, *5*(3), 203-211.

Baiden, P., Den Dunnen, W., & Fallon, B. (2017). Examining the independent effect of social support on unmet mental healthcare needs among Canadians: Findings from a population-based study. *Social Indicators Research*, *130*, 1229-1246.

Bandura, A. (2000). Self-efficacy: The foundation of agency. *Control of Human Behavior, Mental Processes, And Consciousness: Essays in Honor Of the 60th Birthday of August Flammer*, *16*.

Barnett, J. H., Lewis, L., Blackwell, A. D., & Taylor, M. (2014). Early intervention in Alzheimer's disease: a health economic study of the effects of diagnostic timing. *BMC Neurology*, *14*(1), 1-9.

Beals, J., Novins, D. K., Whitesell, N. R., Spicer, P., Mitchell, C. M., Manson, S. M., & American Indian Service Utilization, Psychiatric Epidemiology, Risk and Protective Factors Project Team. (2005). Prevalence of mental disorders and utilization of mental health services in two American Indian reservation populations: Mental health disparities in a national context. *American Journal of Psychiatry*, *162*(9), 1723-1732.

Benjet, C., Bromet, E., Karam, E. G., Kessler, R. C., McLaughlin, K. A., Ruscio, A. M., . . . & Koenen, K. C. (2016). The epidemiology of traumatic event exposure worldwide: results from the World Mental Health Survey Consortium. *Psychological Medicine*, *46*(2), 327-343.

Berge, E. E., Hagen, R., & Øveraas Halvorsen, J. (2020). PTSD relapse in Veterans of Iraq and Afghanistan: A systematic review. *Military Psychology*, *32*(4), 300-312.

Berk, M., Köhler-Forsberg, O., Turner, M., Penninx, B. W., Wrobel, A., Firth, J., . . . & Marx, W. (2023). Comorbidity between major depressive disorder and physical diseases: a comprehensive review of epidemiology, mechanisms and management. *World Psychiatry*, *22*(3), 366-387.

Bertakis, K. D., Azari, R., Helms, L. J., Callahan, E. J., & Robbins, J. A. (2000). Gender differences in the utilization of health care services. *Journal of Family Practice*, *49*(2).

Biazus, T. B., Beraldi, G. H., Tokeshi, L., Rotenberg, L. D. S., Dragioti, E., Carvalho, A. F., . . . & Lafer, B. (2023). All-cause and cause-specific mortality among people with bipolar disorder: a large-scale systematic review and meta-analysis. *Molecular Psychiatry*, 1-17.

Björkenstam, E., Björkenstam, C., Holm, H., Gerdin, B., & Ekselius, L. (2015). Excess cause-specific mortality in in-patient-treated individuals with personality disorder: 25-year nationwide population-based study. *The British Journal of Psychiatry*, *207*(4), 339-345.

Black, D. W., Baumgard, C. H., & Bell, S. E. (1995). A 16-to 45-year follow-up of 71 men with antisocial personality disorder. *Comprehensive Psychiatry*, *36*(2), 130-140.

Blanco, C., Iza, M., Rodríguez-Fernández, J. M., Baca-García, E., Wang, S., & Olfson, M. (2015). Probability and predictors of treatment-seeking for substance use disorders in the US. *Drug and Alcohol Dependence*, *149*, 136-144.

Borges, G., Bagge, C. L., Cherpitel, C. J., Conner, K. R., Orozco, R., & Rossow, I. (2017). A meta-analysis of acute use of alcohol and the risk of suicide attempt. *Psychological Medicine*, *47*(5), 949-957.

Bradley, R., Greene, J., Russ, E., Dutra, L., & Westen, D. (2005). A multidimensional meta-analysis of psychotherapy for PTSD. *American journal of Psychiatry*, *162*(2), 214-227.

Brave Heart, M. Y. H., Lewis-Fernández, R., Beals, J., Hasin, D. S., Sugaya, L., Wang, S., . . . & Blanco, C. (2016). Psychiatric disorders and mental health treatment in American Indians and Alaska Natives: results of the National Epidemiologic Survey on Alcohol and Related Conditions. *Social Psychiatry and Psychiatric Epidemiology, 51*, 1033-1046.

Bridges, A. J., de Arellano, M. A., Rheingold, A. A., Danielson, C. K., & Silcott, L. (2010). Trauma exposure, mental health, and service utilization rates among immigrant and United States-born Hispanic youth: Results from the Hispanic family study. *Psychological Trauma: Theory, Research, Practice, And Policy, 2*(1), 40.

Bruffaerts, R., Demyttenaere, K., Hwang, I., Chiu, W. T., Sampson, N., Kessler, R. C., . . . & Nock, M. K. (2011). Treatment of suicidal people around the world. *The British Journal of Psychiatry, 199*(1), 64-70.

Butler, A. C., Chapman, J. E., Forman, E. M., & Beck, A. T. (2006). The empirical status of cognitive-behavioral therapy: A review of meta-analyses. *Clinical Psychology Review, 26*(1), 17-31.

Byhoff, E., Guardado, R., Xiao, N., Nokes, K., Garg, A., & Tripodis, Y. (2022). Association of unmet social needs with chronic illness: a cross-sectional study. *Population Health Management, 25*(2), 157-163.

Can, A. T., Hermens, D. F., Dutton, M., Gallay, C. C., Jensen, E., Jones, M., . . . & Lagopoulos, J. (2021). Low dose oral ketamine treatment in chronic suicidality: an open-label pilot study. *Translational Psychiatry, 11*(1), 101.

Castillejos, M. C., Huertas, P., Martin, P., & Moreno Kuestner, B. (2021). Prevalence of suicidality in the European general population: a systematic review and meta-analysis. *Archives of Suicide Research, 25*(4), 810-828.

Charlet, K., & Heinz, A. (2017). Harm reduction—a systematic review on effects of alcohol reduction on physical and mental symptoms. *Addiction Biology, 22*(5), 1119-1159.

Charlson, F. J., Baxter, A. J., Dua, T., Degenhardt, L., Whiteford, H. A., & Vos, T. (2015). Excess mortality from mental, neurological and substance use disorders in the Global Burden of Disease Study 2010. *Epidemiology and Psychiatric Sciences, 24*(2), 121-140.

Charney, D. S., Reynolds, C. F., Lewis, L., Lebowitz, B. D., Sunderland, T., Alexopoulos, G. S., . . . & Young, R. C. (2003). Depression and Bipolar Support Alliance consensus statement on the unmet needs in diagnosis and treatment of mood disorders in late life. *Archives of General Psychiatry, 60*(7), 664-672

Chikritzhs, T., & Livingston, M. (2021). Alcohol and the Risk of Injury. *Nutrients, 13*(8), 2777.

Conger, J. A. (2017). The necessary art of persuasion. In *Leadership Perspectives* (pp. 161-172). Routledge.

Correll, C. U., Solmi, M., Croatto, G., Schneider, L. K., Rohani-Montez, S. C., Fairley, L., . . . & Tiihonen, J. (2022). Mortality in people with schizophrenia: a systematic review and meta-analysis of relative risk and aggravating or attenuating factors. *World Psychiatry, 21*(2), 248-271.

Corrigan, P. W. (2015). Challenging the stigma of mental illness: different agendas, different goals. *Psychiatric Services, 66*(12), 1347-1349.

Cruwys, T., Wakefield, J. R., Sani, F., Dingle, G. A., & Jetten, J. (2018). Social isolation predicts frequent attendance in primary care. *Annals of Behavioral Medicine, 52*(10), 817-829.

Davis, L. L., Leon, A. C., Toscano, R., Drebing, C. E., Ward, L. C., Parker, P. E., . . . & Drake, R. E. (2012). A randomized controlled trial of supported employment among veterans with posttraumatic stress disorder. *Psychiatric Services, 63*(5), 464-470.

Degenhardt, L., Bucello, C., Mathers, B., Briegleb, C., Ali, H., Hickman, M., & McLaren, J. (2011). Mortality among regular or dependent users of heroin and other opioids: a systematic review and meta-analysis of cohort studies. *Addiction, 106*(1), 32-51.

Dennis, M. L., Scott, C. K., Funk, R., & Foss, M. A. (2005). The duration and correlates of addiction and treatment careers. *Journal of Substance Abuse Treatment, 28*(2), S51-S62.

de Winter, R. F., Meijer, C., Kool, N., & de Groot, M. H. (2023). Differentiation of suicidal behavior in clinical practice. In *Suicide risk assessment and prevention* (pp. 219-236). Cham: Springer International Publishing.

Dixon, L. B., Holoshitz, Y., & Nossel, I. (2016). Treatment engagement of individuals experiencing mental illness: review and update. *World Psychiatry, 15*(1), 13-20.

Dixon-Gordon, K. L., Turner, B. J., & Chapman, A. L. (2011). Psychotherapy for personality disorders. *International Review of Psychiatry, 23*(3), 282-302.

Dixon-Gordon, K. L., Whalen, D. J., Layden, B. K., & Chapman, A. L. (2015). A systematic review of personality disorders and health outcomes. *Canadian Psychology/Psychologie Canadienne, 56*(2), 168.

Drebing, C.E. (2014). Onset of Vocational Problems and Subsequent Homelessness Among Veterans Enrolled in VA Services. Part of Symposium for (Chair: J. Tsai). '*Homelessness Among Veterans— Current Research on Special Subgroups*' at the Annual Meeting of the American Psychological Association. Washington, DC.

Drebing, C. E., Reilly, E., Henze, K. T., Kelly, M., Russo, A., Smolinsky, J., . . . & Penk, W. E. (2018). Using peer support groups to enhance community integration of veterans in transition. *Psychological Services, 15*(2), 135.

Druss, B. G., & Goldman, H. H. (2018). Integrating health and mental health services: a past and future history. *American Journal of Psychiatry, 175*(12), 1199-1204.

Dupre, M. E., Beck, A. N., & Meadows, S. O. (2009). Marital trajectories and mortality among US adults. *American Journal of Epidemiology, 170*(5), 546–555.

Dutra, L., Stathopoulou, G., Basden, S. L., Leyro, T. M., Powers, M. B., & Otto, M. W. (2008). A meta-analytic review of psychosocial interventions for substance use disorders. *American Journal of Psychiatry, 165*(2), 179-187.

Eassom, E., Giacco, D., Dirik, A., & Priebe, S. (2014). Implementing family involvement in the treatment of patients with psychosis: a systematic review of facilitating and hindering factors. *BMJ Open, 4*(10), e006108.

Eisenberg, D., Gollust, S. E., Golberstein, E., & Hefner, J. L. (2007). Prevalence and correlates of depression, anxiety, and suicidality among university students. *American Journal of Orthopsychiatry, 77*(4), 534-542.

Esang, M., & Ahmed, S. (2018). A closer look at substance use and suicide. *American Journal of Psychiatry Residents' Journal.*

Evans-Lacko, S., Henderson, C., & Thornicroft, G. (2013). Public knowledge, attitudes and behaviour regarding people with mental illness in England 2009-2012. *The British Journal of Psychiatry, 202*(s55), s51-s57.

Ferrari, A. J., Norman, R. E., Freedman, G., Baxter, A. J., Pirkis, J. E., Harris, M. G., . . . & Whiteford, H. A. (2014). The burden attributable to mental and substance use disorders as risk factors for suicide: findings from the Global Burden of Disease Study 2010. *PloS one, 9*(4), e91936.

Fikretoglu, D., Brunet, A., Guay, S., & Pedlar, D. (2007). Mental health treatment seeking by military members with posttraumatic stress disorder: findings on rates, characteristics, and predictors from a nationally representative Canadian military sample. *The Canadian Journal of Psychiatry*, *52*(2), 103-110.

Fischer, E. P., McSweeney, J. C., Wright, P., Cheney, A., Curran, G. M., Henderson, K., & Fortney, J. C. (2016). Overcoming barriers to sustained engagement in mental health care: perspectives of rural veterans and providers. *The Journal of Rural Health*, *32*(4), 429-438.

Fok, M. L. Y., Hayes, R. D., Chang, C. K., Stewart, R., Callard, F. J., & Moran, P. (2012). Life expectancy at birth and all-cause mortality among people with personality disorder. *Journal of Psychosomatic Research*, *73*(2), 104-107.

Frankenburg, F. R., & Zanarini, M. C. (2006). Personality disorders and medical comorbidity. *Current Opinion in Psychiatry*, *19*(4), 428-431.

Freedman, J., & Combs, G. (1996). *Doing Narrative Therapy*. WW Norton & Company.

Furnham, A., & Swami, V. (2018). Mental health literacy: A review of what it is and why it matters. *International Perspectives in Psychology: Research, Practice, Consultation*, *7*(4), 240.

Fusar-Poli, P., Cappucciati, M., Bonoldi, I., Hui, L. C., Rutigliano, G., Stahl, D. R., . . . & McGuire, P. K. (2016). Prognosis of brief psychotic episodes: a meta-analysis. *JAMA Psychiatry*, *73*(3), 211-220.

Gallegos, A. M., Streltzov, N. A., & Stecker, T. (2016). Improving treatment engagement for returning operation enduring freedom and operation Iraqi freedom veterans with posttraumatic stress disorder, depression, and suicidal ideation. *The Journal of Nervous and Mental Disease*, *204*(5), 339-343.

Gardner, L., and Leshner, G. (2016). The role of narrative and other-referencing in attenuating psychological reactance to diabetes self-care messages. *Health Communication.* 31, 738–751.

Glei, D. A., & Preston, S. H. (2020). Estimating the impact of drug use on US mortality, 1999-2016. *PLoS One, 15*(1), e0226732.

Goldberg, S. B., Simpson, T. L., Lehavot, K., Katon, J. G., Chen, J. A., Glass, J. E., . . . & Fortney, J. C. (2019). Mental health treatment delay: A comparison among civilians and veterans of different service eras. *Psychiatric Services, 70*(5), 358-366.

Gorman, J.A., Scoglio, A.A.J., Smolinsky, J., Russo, A., Drebing, C.E. (2018) Veteran Coffee Socials: A Community-Building Strategy for Enhancing Community Integration of Veterans in Transition from Military to Civilian Life. *Community Mental Health Journal, 54,* 1189-1197.

Gradman, T. J., Thompson, L. W., & Gallagher-Thompson, D. (2013). Personality disorders and treatment outcome. In *Personality disorders in older adults* (pp. 69-94). Routledge.

Granfield, R., & Cloud, W. (1996). The elephant that no one sees: Natural recovery among middle-class addicts. *Journal of Drug Issues, 26*(1), 45-61.

Grant, B. F., Saha, T. D., Ruan, W. J., Goldstein, R. B., Chou, S. P., Jung, J., . . . & Hasin, D. S. (2016). Epidemiology of DSM-5 drug use disorder: Results from the National Epidemiologic Survey on Alcohol and Related Conditions–III. *JAMA Psychiatry, 73*(1), 39-47.

Gronholm, P. C., Thornicroft, G., Laurens, K. R., & Evans-Lacko, S. (2017). Mental health-related stigma and pathways to care for people at risk of psychotic disorders or experiencing first-episode psychosis: a systematic review. *Psychological Medicine, 47*(11), 1867-1879.

Grzywacz, J. G., & Fuqua, J. (2000). The social ecology of health: Leverage points and linkages. *Behavioral Medicine, 26*(3), 101-115.

Hartley, R. D., & Baldwin, J. M. (2019). Waging war on recidivism among justice-involved veterans: An impact evaluation of a large urban veterans' treatment court. *Criminal Justice Policy Review, 30*(1), 52-78.

Hauenstein, E. J., Petterson, S., Merwin, E., Rovnyak, V., Heise, B., & Wagner, D. (2006). Rurality, gender, and mental health treatment. *Family and Community Health*, 169-185.

Have, M. T., De Graaf, R., Van Dorsselaer, S., Verdurmen, J., Van' t Land, H., Vollebergh, W., & Beekman, A. (2009). Incidence and course of suicidal ideation and suicide attempts in the general population. *The Canadian Journal of Psychiatry, 54*(12), 824-833.

Henderson, R. C., Williams, P., Gabbidon, J., Farrelly, S., Schauman, O., Hatch, S., . . . & MIRIAD Study Group. (2015). Mistrust of mental health services: ethnicity, hospital admission and unfair. *Epidemiology and Psychiatric Sciences, 24*(3), 258-265.

Hoglund, M. W., & Schwartz, R. M. (2014). Mental health in deployed and nondeployed veteran men and women in comparison with their civilian counterparts. *Military Medicine, 179*(1), 19-25.

Holdsambeck, L. (2021). Self-Reliance and Self-Efficacy as Determinants of Mental Health Treatment Seeking Intention in a Sample of Student Service Members/Veterans.

Holt-Lunstad, J., Smith, T. B., Baker, M., Harris, T., & Stephenson, D. (2015). Loneliness and social isolation as risk factors for mortality: a meta-analytic review. *Perspectives on Psychological Science, 10*(2), 227-237.

Holzer, K. J., & Vaughn, M. G. (2017). Antisocial personality disorder in older adults: A critical review. *Journal of Geriatric Psychiatry and Neurology, 30*(6), 291-302.

Honegger, L. N. (2015). Does the evidence support the case for mental health courts? A review of the literature. *Law and Human Behavior, 39*(5), 478.

Humphreys, K. (2015). Addiction treatment professionals are not the gatekeepers of recovery. *Substance Use & Misuse, 50*(8-9), 1024-1027.

Humphreys, K., & Moos, R. H. (2007). Encouraging posttreatment self-help group involvement to reduce demand for continuing care services: two-year clinical and utilization outcomes. *Focus, 5*(2), 193-198.

Jennings, K. S., Cheung, J. H., Britt, T. W., Goguen, K. N., Jeffirs, S. M., Peasley, A. L., & Lee, A. C. (2015). How are perceived stigma, self-stigma, and self-reliance related to treatment-seeking? A three-path model. *Psychiatric Rehabilitation Journal, 38*(2), 109.

Joyce, K., Thompson, A., & Marwaha, S. (2016). Is treatment for bipolar disorder more effective earlier in illness course? A comprehensive literature review. *International Journal of Bipolar Disorders, 4*(1), 1-9.

Kessler, R. C., Berglund, P., Demler, O., Jin, R., Merikangas, K. R., & Walters, E. E. (2005). Lifetime prevalence and age-of-onset distributions of DSM-IV disorders in the National Comorbidity Survey Replication. *Archives of General Psychiatry, 62*(6), 593-602.

Kessler, R. C., Olfson, M., & Berglund, P. A. (1998). Patterns and predictors of treatment contact after first onset of psychiatric disorders. *American Journal of Psychiatry, 155*(1), 62-69.

Kirchner, J. E., Booth, B. M., Owen, R. R., Elizabeth Lancaster, A., & Richard Smith, G. (2000). Predictors of patient entry into alcohol treatment after initial diagnosis. *The Journal of Behavioral Health Services & Research, 27*(3), 339-346.

Klingemann, H., Sobell, M. B., & Sobell, L. C. (2010). Continuities and changes in self-change research. *Addiction, 105*(9), 1510-1518.

Kohlberg, L., & Hersh, R. H. (1977). Moral development: A review of the theory. *Theory Into Practice*, 53-59.

Kroenke, K., Spitzer, R. L., Williams, J. B., Monahan, P. O., & Löwe, B. (2007). Anxiety disorders in primary care: prevalence, impairment, comorbidity, and detection. *Annals of Internal Medicine, 146*(5), 317-325.

Kutcher, S., & Wei, Y. (2012). Mental health and the school environment: secondary schools, promotion and pathways to care. *Current Opinion in Psychiatry, 25*(4), 311-316.

Larsen, T. K., McGlashan, T. H., & Moe, L. C. (1996). First-episode schizophrenia: I. Early course parameters. *Schizophrenia Bulletin, 22*(2), 241-256.

Lawrence, E. M., Rogers, R. G., Zajacova, A., & Wadsworth, T. (2019). Marital happiness, marital status, health, and longevity. *Journal of Happiness Studies, 20*(5), 1539-1561.

Ledesma, F., Buti, M., Domínguez-Hernández, R., Casado, M. Á., & Esteban, R. (2020). Is the universal population Hepatitis C virus screening a cost-effective strategy? A systematic review of the economic evidence. *Revista Española de Quimioterapia, 33*(4), 240.

Lewis, C., Roberts, N. P., Gibson, S., & Bisson, J. I. (2020). Dropout from psychological therapies for post-traumatic stress disorder (PTSD) in adults: Systematic review and meta-analysis. *European Journal of Psychotraumatology, 11*(1), 1709709.

Li, Z., Page, A., Martin, G., & Taylor, R. (2011). Attributable risk of psychiatric and socio-economic factors for suicide from individual-level, population-based studies: a systematic review. *Social Science & Medicine, 72*(4), 608-616.

Littell, J. H., & Girvin, H. (2002). Stages of change: A critique. *Behavior Modification, 26*(2), 223-273.

Liu, R. T., Bettis, A. H., & Burke, T. A. (2020). Characterizing the phenomenology of passive suicidal ideation: a systematic review and meta-analysis of its prevalence, psychiatric comorbidity, correlates, and comparisons with active suicidal ideation. *Psychological Medicine, 50*(3), 367-383.

Lorenzo-Luaces, L. (2015). Heterogeneity in the prognosis of major depression: from the common cold to a highly debilitating and recurrent illness. *Epidemiology and Psychiatric Sciences, 24*(6), 466-472.

Madigan, S. (2011). *Narrative therapy.* American Psychological Association.

Marder, S. R., Essock, S. M., Miller, A. L., Buchanan, R. W., Casey, D. E., Davis, J. M., . . . & Shon, S. (2004). Physical health monitoring of patients with schizophrenia. *American Journal of Psychiatry, 161*(8), 1334-1349.

Matza, L. S., Rajagopalan, K. S., Thompson, C. L., & De Lissovoy, G. (2005). Misdiagnosed patients with bipolar disorder: comorbidities, treatment patterns, and direct treatment costs. *Journal of Clinical Psychiatry, 66*(11), 1432-1440.

McDermott, E., Eastham, R., Hughes, E., Pattinson, E., Johnson, K., Davis, S., . . . & Jenzen, O. (2021). Explaining effective mental health support for LGBTQ+ youth: A meta-narrative review. *SSM-Mental Health, 1*, 100004

McIntyre, R. S., Konarski, J. Z., Soczynska, J. K., Wilkins, K., Panjwani, G., Bouffard, B., . . . & Kennedy, S. H. (2006). Medical comorbidity in bipolar disorder: implications for functional outcomes and health service utilization. *Psychiatric Services, 57*(8), 1140-1144.

Méndez-Bustos, P., Calati, R., Rubio-Ramírez, F., Olié, E., Courtet, P., & Lopez-Castroman, J. (2019). Effectiveness of psychotherapy on suicidal risk: a systematic review of observational studies. *Frontiers in Psychology, 10*, 277.

Miller, W. R., & Rollnick, S. (2012). *Motivational interviewing: Helping people change.* Guilford press.

Miller, W. R., & Rose, G. S. (2015). Motivational interviewing and decisional balance: contrasting responses to client ambivalence. *Behavioural and Cognitive Psychotherapy, 43*(2), 129-141.

Miloyan, B., Bulley, A., Bandeen-Roche, K., Eaton, W. W., & Gonçalves-Bradley, D. C. (2016). Anxiety disorders and all-cause mortality: Systematic review and meta-analysis. *Social Psychiatry and Psychiatric Epidemiology, 51*, 1467-1475.

Moagi, M. M., van Der Wath, A. E., Jiyane, P. M., & Rikhotso, R. S. (2021). Mental health challenges of lesbian, gay, bisexual and transgender people: An integrated literature review. *Health SA Gesondheid, 26*(1).

Moitra, M., Santomauro, D., Degenhardt, L., Collins, P. Y., Whiteford, H., Vos, T., & Ferrari, A. (2021). Estimating the risk of suicide associated with mental disorders: A systematic review and meta-regression analysis. *Journal of Psychiatric Research, 137*, 242-249.

Moloney, M. E. (2017). 'Sometimes, it's easier to write the prescription': physician and patient accounts of the reluctant medicalization of sleeplessness. *Sociology of Health & Illness, 39*(3), 333-348.

Monahan, J., Redlich, A. D., Swanson, J., Robbins, P. C., Appelbaum, P. S., Petrila, J., . . . & McNiel, D. E. (2005). Use of leverage to improve adherence to psychiatric treatment in the community. *Psychiatric Services, 56*(1), 37-44.

Moore, S. A., Dowdy, E., Hinton, T., DiStefano, C., & Greer, F. W. (2022). Moving toward implementation of universal mental health screening by examining attitudes toward school-based practices. *Behavioral Disorders, 47*(3), 166-175.

Moos, R. H., & Moos, B. S. (2007). Treated and untreated alcohol-use disorders: Course and predictors of remission and relapse. *Evaluation Review, 31*(6), 564-584.

Morgan, C., Lappin, J., Heslin, M., Donoghue, K., Lomas, B., Reininghaus, U., . . . & Dazzan, P. (2014). Reappraising the long-term course and outcome of psychotic disorders: the AESOP-10 study. *Psychological Medicine, 44*(13), 2713-2726.

Moyer-Gusé, E. (2008). Toward a theory of entertainment persuasion: explaining the persuasive effects of entertainment-education messages. *Communication. Theory* 18, 407–425.

Mustanski, B. S., Garofalo, R., & Emerson, E. M. (2010). Mental health disorders, psychological distress, and suicidality in a diverse sample of lesbian, gay, bisexual, and transgender youths. *American Journal of Public Health, 100*(12), 2426-2432

Nery-Fernandes, F., Quarantini, L. C., Guimarães, J. L., de Oliveira, I. R., Koenen, K. C., Kapczinski, F., & Miranda-Scippa, Â. (2012). Is there an association between suicide attempt and delay of initiation of mood stabilizers in bipolar I disorder? *Journal of Affective Disorders, 136*(3), 1082-1087.

Nichter, B., Stein, M. B., Norman, S. B., Hill, M. L., Straus, E., Haller, M., & Pietrzak, R. H. (2021). Prevalence, correlates, and treatment of suicidal behavior in US military veterans: Results from the 2019–2020 National Health and Resilience in Veterans Study. *The Journal of Clinical Psychiatry, 82*(5), 35870.

Olfson, M., Blanco, C., Wall, M. M., Liu, S. M., & Grant, B. F. (2019). Treatment of common mental disorders in the United States: results from the National Epidemiologic Survey on Alcohol and Related Conditions-III. *The Journal of Clinical Psychiatry, 80*(3), 21534.

Olfson, M., Guardino, M., Struening, E., Schneier, F. R., Hellman, F., & Klein, D. F. (2000). Barriers to the treatment of social anxiety. *American Journal of Psychiatry, 157*(4), 521-527.

Olsson, S., Hensing, G., Burström, B., & Löve, J. (2021). Unmet need for mental healthcare in a population sample in Sweden: a cross-sectional study of inequalities based on gender, education, and country of birth. *Community Mental Health Journal, 57*(3), 470-481.

Peralta, V., García de Jalón, E., Moreno-Izco, L., Peralta, D., Janda, L., Sánchez-Torres, A. M., . . . & SEGPEPs Group Ballesteros A Gil-Berrozpe G Hernández R Lorente R Fañanás L Papiol S Ribeiro M Rosero A Zandio M. (2022). Long-term outcomes of first-admission psychosis: a naturalistic 21-year follow-up study of symptomatic, functional and personal recovery and their baseline predictors. *Schizophrenia Bulletin, 48*(3), 631-642.

Possemato, K., Johnson, E. M., Wray, L. O., Webster, B., & Stecker, T. (2018). The implementation and testing of a referral management system to address barriers to treatment seeking among primary care veterans with PTSD. *Psychological Services, 15*(4), 457.

Price, R. K., Risk, N. K., & Spitznagel, E. L. (2001). Remission from drug abuse over a 25-year period: patterns of remission and treatment use. *American Journal of Public Health, 91*(7), 1107.

Prochaska, J. O., & DiClemente, C. C. (1986). Toward a comprehensive model of change. In *Treating addictive behaviors: Processes of change* (pp. 3-27). Boston, MA: Springer US.

Quadri, S., Kanji, M., Naing, N., & Huqh, M. (2021). Transtheoretical Model of Behavioural Change. *International Journal of Pharmaceutical Research (09752366), 13*(2).

Ramsawh, H. J., Raffa, S. D., Edelen, M. O., Rende, R., & Keller, M. B. (2009). Anxiety in middle adulthood: effects of age and time on the 14-year course of panic disorder, social phobia and generalized anxiety disorder. *Psychological Medicine, 39*(4), 615-624.

Randles, R., & Finnegan, A. (2021). Veteran help-seeking behaviour for mental health issues: a systematic review. *BMJ Military Health.*

Reczek, C., Thomeer, M. B., Gebhardt-Kram, L., & Umberson, D. (2020). "Go see somebody": How spouses promote mental health care. *Society and Mental Health*, *10*(1), 80-96.

Rehm J, Taylor B, Mohapatra S, Irving H, Baliunas D, Patra J, Roerecke M (2010). Alcohol as a risk factor for liver 138 F. J. Charlson et al. https://doi.org/10.1017/S2045796014000687 Published online by Cambridge University Press cirrhosis: a systematic review and meta-analysis. *Drug and Alcohol Review 29*, 437–445.

Reneses, B., Munoz, E., & Lopez-Ibor, J. J. (2009). Factors predicting drop-out in community mental health centres. *World Psychiatry*, *8*(3), 173.

Rens, E., Michielsen, J., Dom, G., Remmen, R., & Van den Broeck, K. (2022). Clinically assessed and perceived unmet mental health needs, health care use and barriers to care for mental health problems in a Belgian general population sample. *BMC Psychiatry*, *22*(1), 1-13.

Roberts, A.L.; Kubzansky, L.D.; Chibnik, L.B.; Rimm, E.B.; & Koenen, K.C. (2020). Association of Posttraumatic Stress and Depressive Symptoms with Mortality in Women. *JAMA Netw Open*. 2020;3(12): e2027935.

Rogler, L.H. & Cortes, D. E. (1993). Help-seeking pathways: a unifying concept in mental health care. *American Journal of Psychiatry, 150*(4),554-561.

Ruijten, P. A. (2021). The similarity-attraction paradigm in persuasive technology: Effects of system and user personality on evaluations and persuasiveness of an interactive system. *Behaviour & Information Technology*, *40*(8), 734-746.

Ruiz, F., Burgo-Black, L., Hunt, S. C., Miller, M., & Spelman, J. F. (2023). A practical review of suicide among veterans: preventive and proactive measures for health care institutions and providers. *Public Health Reports*, *138*(2), 223-231.

Salzer, M. S., Brusilovskiy, E., & Townley, G. (2018). National estimates of recovery-remission from serious mental illness. *Psychiatric Services, 69*(5), 523-528.

SAMSHA. (2024a, January 10). SAMHSA's Working Definition of Recovery https://store.samhsa.gov/sites/defautl/files/pep12-recdef.pdfr.

SAMSHA (2024b, January 10). Peer Support Workers for those in Recovery | SAMHSA. Httpe://www.samhsa.gov/brss-tacs/recovery-suport-tools/peers.

Santiago PN, Ursano RJ, Gray CL, Pynoos RS, Spiegel D, Lewis-Fernandez R, Friedman MJ, Fullerton CS. (2013). A systematic review of PTSD prevalence and trajectories in DSM-5 defined trauma exposed populations: Intentional and non-intentional traumatic events. *PLoS ONE, 8*(4): e59236.

Saeed, S. A., & Bruce, T. J. (1998). Panic disorder: effective treatment options. *American Family Physician, 57*(10), 2405-2412.

Sareen, J., Jagdeo, A., Cox, B. J., Clara, I., ten Have, M., Belik, S. L., . . . & Stein, M. B. (2007). Perceived barriers to mental health service utilization in the United States, Ontario, and the Netherlands. *Psychiatric Services, 58*(3), 357-364.

Sayers, S. L., Hess, T. H., Whitted, P., Straits-Tröster, K. A., & Glynn, S. M. (2021). Coaching Into Care: Veterans Affairs Telephone-Based Service for Concerned Family Members of Military Veterans. *Psychiatric Services, 72*(1), 107-109.

Schneider, R. A., Chen, S. Y., Lungu, A., & Grasso, J. R. (2020). Treating suicidal ideation in the context of depression. *BMC Psychiatry, 20*(1), 1-5.

Schopman SM, Ten Have M, van Balkom AJ, de Graaf R, & Batelaan NM. (2021). Course trajectories of anxiety disorders: Results from a 6-year follow-up in a general population study. *Australian and New Zealand Journal of Psychiatry, 55*(11):1049-1057.

Schrader, C., & Ross, A. (2021). A review of PTSD and current treatment strategies. *Missouri Medicine, 118*(6), 546.

Scott, J., Colom, F., & Vieta, E. (2007). A meta-analysis of relapse rates with adjunctive psychological therapies compared to usual psychiatric treatment for bipolar disorders. *International Journal of Neuropsychopharmacology, 10*(1), 123-129.

Shen, L. (2010). Mitigating psychological reactance: the role of message-induced empathy in persuasion. *Human Communication Research,* 36, 397–422.

Shen, L. (2011). The effectiveness of empathy-versus fear-arousing antismoking PSAs. *Health Communication,* 26, 404–415.

Shiner, B., Riblet, N., Westgate, C. L., Young-Xu, Y., & Watts, B. V. (2016). Suicidal ideation is associated with all-cause mortality. *Military Medicine, 181*(9), 1040-1045.

Simonelli, A., & Parolin, M. (2020). Dependent personality disorder. In *Encyclopedia of personality and individual differences* (pp. 1048-1059). Cham: Springer International Publishing.

Solomon, P. (2004). Peer support/peer provided services underlying processes, benefits and critical ingredients. *Psychiatric Rehabilitation Journal, 27*(4), 392–401.

Stecker, T., McHugo, G., Xie, H., Whyman, K., & Jones, M. (2014). RCT of a brief phone-based CBT intervention to improve PTSD treatment utilization by returning service members. *Psychiatric Services, 65*(10), 1232-1237.

Stevenson, B. J., Calixte, R. M., Peckham, A. D., Degeis, M., Teravainen, T. S., Chamberlin, E. S., & Mueller, L. (2023). Preventing job loss and functional decline: Description and demonstration of the Veterans Health Administration supported Employment: Engage and Keep (SEEK) program. *Psychological Services.*

Stone, D. M., Jones, C. M., & Mack, K. A. (2021). Changes in suicide rates—United States, 2018–2019. *Morbidity and Mortality Weekly Report, 70*(8), 261.

Steele, L. S., Daley, A., Curling, D., Gibson, M. F., Green, D. C., Williams, C. C., & Ross, L. E. (2017). LGBT identity, untreated depression, and unmet need for mental health services by sexual minority women and trans-identified people. *Journal of Women's Health, 26*(2), 116-127

Steele, L., Dewa, C., & Lee, K. (2007). Socioeconomic status and self-reported barriers to mental health service use. *The Canadian Journal of Psychiatry, 52*(3), 201-206.

Stone, D. M., Jones, C. M., & Mack, K. A. (2021). Changes in suicide rates—United States, 2018–2019. *Morbidity and Mortality Weekly Report, 70*(8), 261.

Strike, C., Rhodes, A. E., Bergmans, Y., & Links, P. (2006). Fragmented pathways to care: The experiences of suicidal men. *Crisis, 27*(1), 31-38.

Suárez-Pinilla, P., Pérez-Herrera, M., Suárez-Pinilla, M., Medina-Blanco, R., López-García, E., Artal-Simón, J. Á., & de Santiago-Díaz, A. I. (2020). Recurrence of suicidal thoughts and behaviors during one year of follow-up: An exploratory study. *Psychiatry Research, 288*, 112988.

Sullivan-Baca, E., Rehman, R., & Haneef, Z. (2023). An update on the healthy soldier effect in US Veterans. *Military Medicine, 188*(9-10), 3199-3204.

Thornicroft, G., Chatterji, S., Evans-Lacko, S., Gruber, M., Sampson, N., Aguilar-Gaxiola, S., . . . & Kessler, R. C. (2017). Undertreatment of people with major depressive disorder in 21 countries. *The British Journal of Psychiatry, 210*(2), 119-124.

Timko, C., Moos, R. H., Finney, J. W., & Lesar, M. D. (2000). Long-term outcomes of alcohol use disorders: comparing untreated individuals with those in alcoholics anonymous and formal treatment. *Journal of Studies on Alcohol, 61*(4), 529-540.

Toneatto, T., Sobell, L. C., Sobell, M. B., & Rubel, E. (1999). Natural recovery from cocaine dependence. *Psychology of Addictive Behaviors, 13*(4), 259.

Tucker, J. A., Chandler, S. D., & Witkiewitz, K. (2020). Epidemiology of recovery from alcohol use disorder. *Alcohol Research: Current Reviews, 40*(3).

Vigo, D., Thornicroft, G., & Atun, R. (2016). Estimating the true global burden of mental illness. *The Lancet Psychiatry, 3*(2), 171-178.

Walker, E. R., Cummings, J. R., Hockenberry, J. M., & Druss, B. G. (2015). Insurance status, use of mental health services, and unmet need for mental health care in the United States. *Psychiatric Services, 66*(6), 578-584.

Walters, G. D. (2000). Spontaneous remission from alcohol, tobacco, and other drug abuse: Seeking quantitative answers to qualitative questions. *The American Journal of Drug and Alcohol Abuse, 26*(3), 443-460.

Wang, P. S., Berglund, P. A., Olfson, M., & Kessler, R. C. (2004). Delays in initial treatment contact after first onset of a mental disorder. *Health Services Research, 39*(2), 393-416.

Wang, P. S., Berglund, P., Olfson, M., Pincus, H. A., Wells, K. B., & Kessler, R. C. (2005a). Failure and delay in initial treatment contact after first onset of mental disorders in the National Comorbidity Survey Replication. *Archives of General Psychiatry, 62*(6), 603-613.

Wang, P. S., Lane, M., Olfson, M., Pincus, H. A., Wells, K. B., & Kessler, R. C. (2005b). Twelve-month use of mental health services in the United States: results from the National

Comorbidity Survey Replication. *Archives of General Psychiatry, 62*(6), 629-640.

Watkins, L. E., Sprang, K. R., & Rothbaum, B. O. (2018). Treating PTSD: A review of evidence-based psychotherapy interventions. *Frontiers in Behavioral Neuroscience, 12*, 258.

Wendt, D., & Shafer, K. (2016). Gender and attitudes about mental health help seeking: results from national data. *Health & Social Work, 41*(1), e20-e28.

Wenzel, A. (2012). Modification of core beliefs in cognitive therapy. *Standard and innovative strategies in Cognitive Behavior Therapy*, 17-34.

Westman, J., Wahlbeck, K., Laursen, T. M., Gissler, M., Nordentoft, M., Hällgren, J., . . . & Ösby, U. (2015). Mortality and life expectancy of people with alcohol use disorder in Denmark, Finland and Sweden. *Acta Psychiatrica Scandinavica, 131*(4), 297-306.

White, M., & Epston, D. (1990). *Narrative means to therapeutic ends*. WW Norton & Company.

Whiteford HA, Harris MG, McKeon G, Baxter A, Pennell C, Barendregt JJ, Wang J. (2013). Estimating remission from untreated major depression: a systematic review and meta-analysis. *Psychological Medicine, 43*(8):1569-85.

Witkiewitz, K., Pearson, M. R., Wilson, A. D., Stein, E. R., Votaw, V. R., Hallgren, K. A., . . . & Tucker, J. A. (2020). Can alcohol use disorder recovery include some heavy drinking? A replication and extension up to 9 years following treatment. *Alcoholism: Clinical and Experimental Research, 44*(9), 1862-1874.

Witt, K., Potts, J., Hubers, A., Grunebaum, M. F., Murrough, J. W., Loo, C., . . . & Hawton, K. (2020). Ketamine for suicidal ideation in adults with psychiatric disorders: a systematic review and meta-analysis of treatment trials. *Australian & New Zealand Journal of Psychiatry*, *54*(1), 29-45.

Wittchen, H. U. (1988). Natural course and spontaneous remissions of untreated anxiety disorder: Results of the Munich Follow-up Study (MFS). In I. Hand & H. U. Wittchen (Eds.), *Panic and Phobias*. Berlin: Springer.

Wolitzky-Taylor, K. B., Horowitz, J. D., Powers, M. B., & Telch, M. J. (2008). Psychological approaches in the treatment of specific phobias: A meta-analysis. *Clinical Psychology Review*, *28*(6), 1021-1037.

Worrall, H., Schweizer, R., Marks, E., Yuan, L., Lloyd, C., & Ramjan, R. (2018). The effectiveness of support groups: a literature review. *Mental Health and Social Inclusion*, *22*(2), 85-93.

Wunderink, L., Sytema, S., Nienhuis, F. J., & Wiersma, D. (2009). Clinical recovery in first-episode psychosis. *Schizophrenia Bulletin*, *35*(2), 362-369.

Wyatt, L. C., Ung, T., Park, R., Kwon, S. C., & Trinh-Shevrin, C. (2015). Risk factors of suicide and depression among Asian American, Native Hawaiian, and Pacific Islander youth: A systematic literature review. *Journal of Health Care for the Poor and Underserved*, *26*(2 0), 191.

Yang, K. G., Rodgers, C. R., Lee, E., & Lê Cook, B. (2020). Disparities in mental health care utilization and perceived need among Asian Americans: 2012–2016. *Psychiatric Services*, *71*(1), 21-27.

Yang, J. C., Roman-Urrestarazu, A., McKee, M., & Brayne, C. (2019). Demographic, socioeconomic, and health correlates of unmet need for mental health treatment in the United States, 2002–16: evidence from the national surveys on drug use and health. *International Journal for Equity in Health*, *18*, 1-11.

Yurica, C. L., & DiTomasso, R. A. (2005). Cognitive distortions. *Encyclopedia of Cognitive Behavior Therapy*, 117-122.

Zanarini, M. C., Frankenburg, F. R., Reich, D. B., & Fitzmaurice, G. (2012). Attainment and stability of sustained symptomatic remission and recovery among borderline patients and axis II comparison subjects: a 16-year prospective follow-up study. *The American Journal of Psychiatry, 169*(5), 476.

Zanarini, M. C., Frankenburg, F. R., Reich, D. B., & Fitzmaurice, G. (2012). Attainment and stability of sustained symptomatic remission and recovery among patients with borderline personality disorder and axis II comparison subjects: a 16-year prospective follow-up study. *American Journal of Psychiatry, 169*(5), 476-483.

Ziffra, M. (2021). Panic disorder: a review of treatment options. *Ann Clin Psychiatry, 33*(2), 124-133.

Look For Other Titles in This Series:

The Peer Specialist Pocket Resource for Mental Health & Substance Use Services

Including Peer Specialists in Health Care Settings is one of the most important developments in the past 30 years. The expanded edition of this pocket resource for Peer Specialists is designed to help you serve effectively as a peer while navigating what is often a complex and confusing clinical setting. Chapters include: Dealing with Critical Situations, Creating and Using Good Recovery Stories, Helping Clients Navigate Healthcare and Social Service Systems, Working Successfully in Healthcare & Social Service Agencies, Good Documentation, Dealing with Legal & Ethical Issues.

Leading Peer Support Groups: A Peer Specialist Pocket Resource

While Peer Specialists are often called upon to develop and lead peer support groups, this is often a challenging task. This pocket resource is designed to help Peer Specialists develop and expand their group facilitation skills to help build and facilitate strong healthy peer support groups. Chapters include: Key Skills for Facilitating a Meeting, Understanding and Maintaining Boundaries, Developing a New Group, Dealing with the Difficult Group Members, Legal and Ethical Issues.

www.ingramcontent.com/pod-product-compliance
Lightning Source LLC
Chambersburg PA
CBHW071402150726
48000CB00001B/130